Published in 2023 by Collective Fashion Justice with Heads & Tales an imprint of Hardie Grant Media

Hardie Grant Media (Melbourne)
Building 1, 658 Church Street
Richmond VIC 3121, Australia

www.hardiegrant.com.au

Hardie Grant and Collective Fashion Justice acknowledges the Traditional Owners of the Country
on which we work, the Wurundjeri People of the Kulin Nation and the Gadigal People of the Eora Nation,
and recognises their continuing connection to the land, waters and culture. We pay our respects
to their Elders past and present.

A catalogue record of this book is available from the National Library of Australia

Total Ethics Fashion

ISBN 9781761450259

Designed by Very Good Looking
Printed in Australia by Ellikon Fine Printers

People, our fellow animals and
the planet before profit

Total
Ethics
Fashion

Emma Hakansson

About the author

Emma Hakansson is the founding director of Collective Fashion Justice. She is a writer, an award-winning film director and a passionate advocate for collective liberation. Having always loved fashion, Emma's relationship with the industry first began through modelling followed by creative direction and production, before she became committed to helping transform the industry, how it operates and the values it stands on. Her work and words have been featured across *The Business of Fashion, The Guardian, Forbes, Vogue Business, WWD* and many other publications.

About the organisation

Collective Fashion Justice (CFJ) is a not-for-profit organisation dedicated to creating a total ethics fashion system which prioritises the life and wellbeing of people, our fellow animals and the planet before profit.

CFJ works to create change at a government, industry and citizen level: lobbying for political change, educating the next generation of fashion's thinkers, makers and designers with university partners, consulting with brands, and shifting mainstream mindsets on fashion through film, creative content and awareness-raising campaigns.

Contents

1.
Introducing fashion, and our need for a total ethics fashion system

In 2021, Pantone titled a shade of green with a Leprechaun namesake as one of the leading colours for fall at New York Fashion Week.[1] It was the same year that Bottega Veneta, followed by several other luxury brands, made this intense lime green so popular that no one interested in the industry could miss it.[2, 3] It's now simply called 'Bottega Green'.[3] As Miranda Priestly in *The Devil Wears Prada* told us would happen, that green then trickled down through almost every high street brand – and at a more rapid pace than ever before, as micro-trends pushed out through social media accelerated an already too fast fashion industry.[4–6] This was the greenest thing to happen in fashion for a long time. And that includes any kind of 'green' action for the planet.

Green-washed fashion marketing can easily lead us to believe the industry is far better for the environment than it is. If we don't know how to see through the buzzwordy promises.[7, 8] Clothes made mostly of virgin fossil fuel-based synthetics are labelled something like 'responsible' if some tiny portion is recycled.[9, 10] Brands adding hundreds of new styles to their sites each day call themselves 'conscious' despite the landfill crisis they perpetuate, because those dumping sites are being filled with partly organic cotton clothes.[11] The fur industry still calls wild, native animals 'natural resources',[12] and the leather industry is hellbent on calling itself 'natural' and 'sustainable', while decimating global biodiversity and contributing disproportionately to fashion's climate crisis impacts.[13]

The bulk of work on sustainability in fashion seems to be in marketing, rather than making real change. This kind of deceptive messaging, which intentionally tricks people eager to make better choices into lining corporate pockets, is not helping the planet. Of course, it's not all bad: while they're making some mistakes, a lot of brands are also trying to improve. We're seeing real leaders working for radical action to transform the fashion industry into one which can coexist with the planet, rather than extract from it until there's little left. Science innovators and farmers alike are rethinking fashion materials as we know them. What's more, activists, organisations, some politicians, and educators are working to ensure sorely needed and real, structural, and systemic changes to the fashion industry are made.

But there's still a problem. Our view of sustainability is far from total. So much of the way we talk about sustainability in fashion is incredibly cold – despite the global temperature rise. We talk about the climate, about greenhouse gas emissions, water use, waste, landfills, pollution, chemicals, deforestation and destruction in isolation. We talk about data, life-cycle assessments, analysis frameworks and measurement tools. And we need this stuff. But we also need to talk about sustainability in a way which acknowledges that the reason our current planetary crisis matters is because life matters. 'Nature' in its total form is made up not only of landscapes; forests, grasslands and waterways, but of individuals: animals, including homo sapiens, among so many others we share the Earth with. Protecting our planet must mean protecting us all.

It's time to quit talking about a kind of environmental protection and regeneration which is separate from the wellbeing of those who live in the environment. Indigenous communities have been saying it forever: we cannot continue to see ourselves as separate from nature, should we protect it.

Native American poet, activist and professor Paula Gunn Allen expressed it most clearly: 'It is not a matter of being "close to nature"... Earth is, in a very real sense, the same as our self (or selves)'.[14] When we recognise ourselves as one with nature, the ways in which fashion systemically harms →

individuals becomes more
clearly a part of fashion's
sustainability crisis.

Our human-induced planetary crisis impacts people, and just as much, our mistreatment of people harms the Earth.[15] We see this interconnectedness play out across the fashion industry, and we see it in solutions to this problem, too. For example, it's theorised that ending poverty pay for the people who make our clothes could also combat the climate crisis.[16] While multi-billion dollar brand CEOs,[17] their boards and hired experts ponder how to reduce their environmental impact, a solution sits right in front of them: pay the people who make your clothes enough to live well and you will live well too. Less money will be free to plunder the planet with, meaning that we'll share a habitable planet. Too, while profit margins won't continuously grow, our connection to each other and the Earth we share just might.

'People and planet over profit' is a growing call from climate activists now leaning into these truths but, still, something is missing from the whole. Humans make up just 2.5% of all animal biomass, which is made up of trillions of lives.[18] To talk about protecting nature or the environment in a way that acknowledges sentient life while only talking about 2.5% of such life is absurd. Thinking about it this way, monolithic and vague talk of fashion's contribution to 'biodiversity loss' and how it's bad for the environment is shallow too. 'Biodiversity loss' (or really, 'biodiversity destruction') is, in part, the suffering of billions of wild and native animals, who are dying as a result of habitat and other destruction in current clothing supply chains.[19, 20] Environmental crises are then, even further still, ethical crises.

Life on Earth: the distribution of animal biomass

0.3%
Wild mammals
(0.007 billion
tonnes carbon)

4%
Farmed animals
(0.1 billion tonnes carbon)

2.5%
Humans
(0.06 billion
tonnes carbon)

0.08%
Wild birds
(0.002 billion tonnes carbon)

* Animal biomass not pictured:

Arthropods (42%), **Fish** (29%), **Annelids** (8%), **Molluscs** (8%), **Cnidarians** (4%), **Nematodes** (0.8%).

And there's one more, not so small thing: the animals we breed, farm, exploit and kill make up 4% of all animal biomass.[18] These farmed animals, like the cows, sheep, goats, ducks, crocodiles, raccoon dogs and other species entrapped, exploited and slaughtered in fashion supply chains, are undoubtedly a part of nature, too. While our current system separates them from nature, denies them their nature, even punishes their nature, they remain a part of nature.[21–23] Just as we do, despite the separations from the rest of the Earth that we have built 'for' ourselves. If talking about fashion and sustainability properly means talking about life, and about ethics, we need to talk about animals.

Our current fashion system deems these other-than-human individuals more 'commodity' than 'community' on this planet. This causes them immense suffering,[24] and this suffering permeates outward, presenting itself through exorbitant emissions, land destruction and interlinked human health crises.[20, 25–27] The wellbeing of our planet, of ourselves, and of those we share nature with are inseparable, no matter how hard we try to compartmentalise them.

Fashion's move from green colourings to green action is critical, but it's not going to work unless the environment is something fashion considers holistically. It's not going to work unless we recognise that, just as we cannot sustain environmental degradation as we know it, we cannot sustain injustice. It will fail unless we work for a 'total ethics fashion system'. To work for such a system, we cannot see our planetary crises as separate from our ethical crises. We cannot try to mend part of the fabric of our Earth and think the whole cloth will be preserved.

We need a future-proofed fashion system that works for all of us. We need fashion as art and individuality, rather than as corporate greed. It's time for us to do, dress and create better, to expect more from fashion. To accept nothing less than the creation of a total ethics fashion system: one which prioritises the life and wellbeing of our total environment, we people, our fellow animals, and the planet we share and live as part of. Without total ethics, the future of fashion is not only unacceptably harmful, but unable to sustain itself, unable to coexist with a sustainably living and growing environment.

Fashion which values humans

living wages

socially supportive

empowered
garment workers

e.g.
ethically produced
shoes made of invasive
toad skin

e.g.
ethically made
vegan bags made
of toxic PVC

Total
ethics
fashion

Fashion
which
values
the planet

Fashion
which
values
other animals

slow fashion

e.g. pineapple leaf
leather jacket made
by someone paid
a poverty wage

free from animal skins

low-impact
processes

no animal-derived
glues or dyes

eco-friendly
textiles

free from down,
silk and wool

2.
Where fashion is today

Fashion is seen by some as vapid and unimportant, but this couldn't be less true. Fashion is a way of expression, an art form that allows for identity development and pride, for the carving out of individuality as much as the fostering of culture and history. Fashion can be a joy, an expression of emotion, a symbol. We wear black at funerals, decorate ourselves on special occasions and create common ground through clothing, recognising our similar interests and communities through our dress. I, and so many of us, have used fashion as play, as confident armour, as a means of lifting one's mood or exploring parts of the self we might otherwise be reluctant to tap into. We've adorned ourselves for millennia and fashion is never going away.[1] This is good: a world without fashion would be one of great expressive loss.

Fashion is not only important as an art form, it is also a serious industry with momentous impacts on everything it touches. Not only in its ability to creatively turn the picture of society, but in the physical harms caused by its production. It's estimated that today, over 100 billion garments are made every single year.[2] There's now 8 billion of us humans,[3] so split evenly, that's a little more than one new garment every month. But it's not split evenly. Wealthy nations are buying the most: on average, people in the United States buy a new garment every five days, while Australians buy new clothes more than weekly, and those in the United Kingdom purchase a collective two tonnes per minute.[4–6]

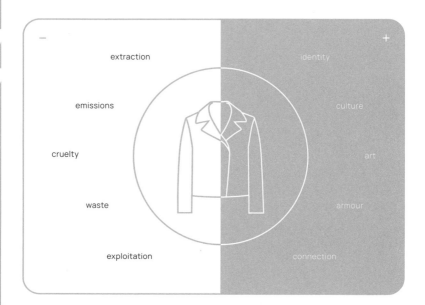

The average global citizen buys 5kg of clothing each year, but across Europe and North America, we're buying as much as 26kg each year.[7, 8] Wealth disparity within such affluent areas also means that those well above the poverty line are probably buying even more.

Meanwhile, it's also reported that around the world, a garbage truck full of textiles is sent to landfill every second.[9] One Chilean desert alone is smothered in tens of thousands of tonnes of unsold and unworn clothes each year – made too quickly for people to keep up with, but breaking down in landfill, releasing methane for far longer, at the expense of the desert's biodiversity.[10, 11] Similarly, at Accra's Kantamanto markets in Ghana, as many as 15 million garments are churned through each week.[12] The garments, referred to as 'dead white man's clothes', are skillfully refurbished when they can be, yet 40% of these clothes end up in flaming piles, floating in seas and dumped on the doorsteps of vulnerable communities who played no part in this mess.[13, 14]

While the exact reported number of garments discarded and burned might vary across datasets – and we need to better understand the specifics of this global problem – anyone paying attention recognises this challenge as a mammoth one. And here's something else we know for sure: fewer and fewer of us actually see fashion as a kind of art anymore. Cultivating a personal sense of style is discouraged by an industry fuelled by an obsession with newness, where what's hot is replicated by brand after brand and diversity of creativity is in decline, even danger. Clothing used to be connected to community – think of the local tailors, the sewing and knitting circles we've lost – to heritage, to culture, to family, ceremony and art. Our current fashion system is losing its roots, homogenising how we dress. The industry we've created today is ravenous, eating away at its own cultural significance, at the planet, at us all.

The way fashion exists today doesn't just come with cultural loss, but too often at the expense of most of what is touched in the making of clothes: many forests, people, wild and farmed animals, waterways, even the air. Supply chains which create clothes are now fragmented; many of their different tiers (stages where different parts of the clothes-making process occur) are often totally untraceable not just to those buying these clothes, but even to many of the brands making them.[15] In the invisibility, destruction and exploitation run amok. To understand this, let's look at two supply chains making clothes: one producing fast fashion, and another, what we consider to be luxurious. These supply chains may seem overwhelmingly destructive, but unfortunately, this is the norm across far too much of the industry.

This is a fast fashion supply chain.
It's making a dress.

Tier four: Where raw materials are made

Raw materials are those made into fabrics and textiles. For cotton, it's a farm.
For leather, a ranch. For viscose, a forest (soon to be cut down), and for synthetics
like polyester, an oil mine. 62% of clothes are made from synthetic materials
now.[16] That means those clothes are plastic and, generally, that they're derived
from fossil fuels. Ultra-fast fashion brands haven't got the memo on a global shift
beyond fossil fuel extraction and use being necessary to prevent climate crisis
(or they have, but they don't care).[17] Fashion's annual use of oil for fabric production
exceeds that of all of Spain.[18]

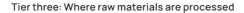

Tier three: Where raw materials are processed

With next to no transparency, modern slavery on ships lugging crude oil around
the world brings in profits for companies with little idea of the exploitation
they're tied to,[19] or the soaring high planetary and human cost of that shiny
satin dress. Most synthetic fibres are made in China and other Asian countries,[18]
where – while ethical labour does exist – modern slavery risks are higher
than those of many other nations.[19] After electronic devices, garments
are at the highest risk of being associated with modern slavery when imported
into G20 countries.[19] This is in part due to the complex and murky supply chains
behind them, which render exploitation near impossible to trace. These facilities,
full of people plasticising, melting and spinning oil into yarn, are also usually
energy-intensive and run on coal power.[18]

Tier two: Where finished materials are made

Spun plastic yarn is dyed and finished into fabrics printed with ironically natural iconography;[21] floral depictions are more appealing than the mines the material came from. Locked in time, the short-lived blooming of a flower will be long outlasted by a material which, on finishing, can take from 20 to 200 years to break down into the Earth,[22] leaching chemicals into the soil that in turn compromise the promise of further flowering. In more scientific terms, 'polyester microplastic fibres in soil increase nitrogen loss via leaching and decrease plant biomass'.[23]

Tier one: Where materials are made into garments

Most people who make clothes do so in China, Bangladesh and Viet Nam,[24] following the shuttering of most western local manufacturing in a capitalistic race to the bottom. In a neocolonial, racist system, it's easier to exploit and underpay people of colour who live overseas, where you don't need to see their plight. Forced and bonded labour, physical, sexual and verbal violence are all reported in this stage of fashion production.[25] As little as 2–10% of garment workers are paid a living wage for their work, keeping the vast majority of these people – mostly women – in a cycle of poverty where their basic needs cannot be met.[26-28] The ultra-fastest of fast fashion brands today, SHEIN, works mostly with synthetic materials and pays pennies per garment to people who work for 18 hours at a time.[29] When faster means more funds for those profiting, people already working long hours to make ends meet are incentivised towards speed, not quality, and so sewing techniques for long-lasting clothes aren't utilised.

This is a luxury fashion supply chain.
It's making a handbag.

Tier four: Raw materials

It's convenient to picture healthy green hills and happy grazing cows as the beginning of the leather supply chain, but it's also inaccurate.[30] Those rolling green hills and grassy pastures often used to be thick, lively forests and now they're barren of biodiversity. While this isn't a problem exclusive to Brazilian leather production, luxury fashion tied to the Amazon biome is also tied to deforestation, to land-grabbing, and even to forced labour, where people are kept in 'slave-like' conditions, working in jobs that are, no matter the country of origin, brutal.[30-32] Think calves ripped from their mothers' sides, standard mutilation practices with sharp knives and metal tools, hot irons and living animals reduced to lifeless 'stock'.[32] If we could see methane, these places would be enveloped with clouds of it, warming the climate while the land below degrades, and water is drunk up and eutrophied by running off manure filled with phosphorus.[30]

Tier three: Raw materials processing

What's a sterile factory for synthetics is a slaughterhouse for leather.[33] The 'raw material' of leather is skin, pulled, fatty and thick, off the carcasses of the hanging and now silent dead, before being sold to the fashion industry as a valuable co-product for further processing.[32] While slaughterhouses report major financial loss when skins don't sell (as alternative material popularity rises),[32] the loss of life is far more significant, and it compounds. Slaughterhouse workers also face a kind of loss, a loss of self, so much more likely are they to face perpetration-induced traumatic stress and its symptoms, in what Yale Health called 'the psychological consequences of the act of killing'.[34]

Trauma turned to more trauma, the pattern repeats again when communities surrounding slaughterhouses face higher risks of violent crimes, including rape,[35] all the while risking ill-health from bloody and biohazardous slaughterhouse pollution.[31]

Tier two: Finished materials

Cow skin leather boots would rot on our feet if it weren't for the tanning process which exists to render the organic inorganic.[30] No longer effectively biodegradable after the process,[36] as many as 170 unique chemicals are used in tanning and can harm surrounding communities, environments and wildlife.[37] The people who work with these carcinogenic chemicals, like chromium (used in 90% of leather processing) and formaldehyde,[30] face higher cancer rates across the globe.[31] While dangerous tannery work across China, India, and Bangladesh is more widely known, even in the Italian tanneries we may think of as luxurious (if we think of them at all), people are often exploited. Meagre pay, dangerous, even deadly jobs and illegally unjust contracts are more likely for migrants in Italy, where fashion and racism mix dangerously once again.[31] Mixed, as the substances used to coat and finish leather are often, with plastic, whether or not the label tells us so.[30]

Tier one: Garment making

The clues of exploitation are right in front of you when it comes to cheap dresses from fast fashion brands: how could the person who made it be paid fairly when the dress sells for $10? The issues wrapped up with far too much of the luxury fashion industry's processes are harder to catch; surely something sold for hundreds, if not thousands, of dollars wouldn't be made by a person paid a couple of dollars an hour? Not so sure, as again, even behind famed 'Made in Italy' labels, leather goods from luxury brands have been stitched by the hands of migrants being made into machines for a couple bucks.[31]

Some of the problems presented in these supply chains can be minimised and removed: modern slavery can and must be eradicated, pollution better captured and the most cruel treatment of individuals eliminated. Even then, both of these supply chains have rotting harm at their core. There's no 'clean' oil, no needless yet 'humane' slaughter, no escaping the inherent, unjust inefficiency at best and cruel destructiveness at worst in the making of dresses and shoes like these.

While brands desperately feed an endlessly growing capitalist machine as they struggle to stay on top, they perpetuate a system that will eventually drain even them, no matter how rich they become. Because feeding our current fashion system means starving the planet, starving the people who make our clothes and disembowelling the bellies of those we think would look better on our feet and slung over our shoulders.

When we're so far from any true sense of sustainability and ethics in so much of fashion, the conversations we do have about these things tend to stay confined within the bounds and boxes of the current, rampaging system.

And that means we are failing to talk about these things properly at all.

3.
How we view fashion and sustainability

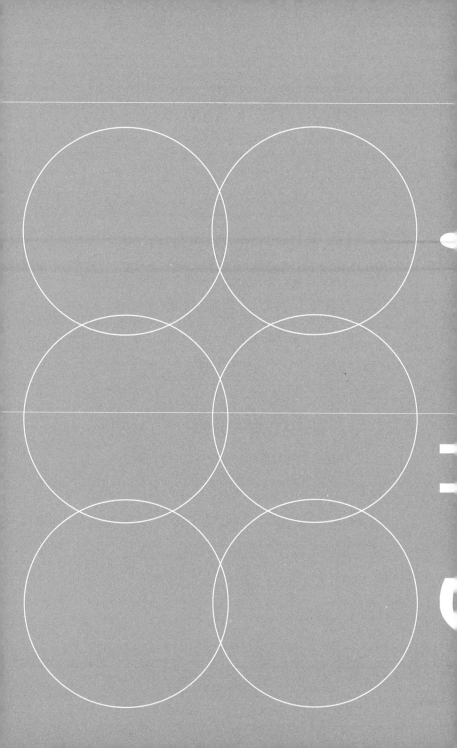

There is no way to sustain our current fashion system, so sustainable fashion cannot exist within the industry today.

The materials we frequently use and wear are depleting the planet, often even when coming to us with promises of being 'natural', 'responsible' or 'conscious'. Too, the energy our industry is fuelled with is far from green.[1]

Materials matter. Hugely so. As a single impact category, raw material production is responsible for more emissions than any other in the industry, as much as 38%.[2] This part of fashion is also most responsible for biodiversity destruction and a host of other environmental harms.[3, 4] If we look at the data, and listen to IPCC recommendations and calls from leading scientists, it's clear that a fashion industry which wants to exist in alignment with the Earth, limiting its impact on it as much as possible, must accept that the production of both fossil fuel-based and animal-derived materials must be moved beyond.[5-8]

Within environmentally minded spaces, it's generally easier to convince people of the first part. We're facing ecosystem collapse, and as hard as BP tried to ensure otherwise, we know fossil fuel extraction is a dangerous foe we must be rid of.[9] It's the leading cause of the climate crisis and must be urgently phased out, as confirmed by the UN's Intergovernmental Panel on Climate Change (IPCC).[5, 10] Less widely acknowledged, the IPCC also states that a switch to animal-free product alternatives would result in a 'substantial reduction' of greenhouse gas emissions, and that methane emissions specifically – largely caused by animal production systems – have contributed 0.5 of our 1.1°C of global warming so far – with the global consensus being that we must work to curb warming before we reach 1.5°C.[11-14] The UN's Food and Agriculture Organization has also long stated that farmed animal production is 'one of the most significant contributors to today's most serious environmental problems' and that 'urgent action is required to remedy the situation'.[15]

Even despite this scientific consensus amongst leading experts, convincing people of the animal side of fashion's required transformation continues to be much harder than that of oil-based synthetics. This is in large part thanks to fallacies of the 'natural', and lobbying by industries which looked to the likes of Exxon's cover-ups as inspiration, not something wicked.[9, 16]

The fallacy of the natural

If something is 'natural', it's derived from nature, the physical world around us, not made by we humans. Appeals to nature imply that if something is 'natural' then it must be 'good', and vice versa. But plenty of things fall into the 'natural' and 'bad' categories alike: deadly viruses that have killed millions of people, for example. When people argue that wool is 'natural' and therefore 'good' for fashion, they rely on this same premise, but they miss a few things. While it's true that the hairs which grow off the bodies of animals are natural, and that sheep are raised outdoors in the environment, everything else about the wool industry is human-designed and controlled.[17]

'Natural' confused for 'sustainable'

Domesticated merino sheep are the selectively bred descendants of mouflon, who have lost their naturally shedded, outer fur layer in place of an unnaturally thick wool layer which won't fall out.[17] In fashion's wool production, the matter of which animals breed, which animals die and which bloodlines continue are decisions designed by the industry for profit. These manipulated, commodified animals often stand on monopastural lands which were once full of abundantly biodiverse plant and animal life.[17, 18] Now it's just green grass and sheep, and millions of them: 70 million in Australia alone, over 1 billion globally.[18] This scale cannot be remedied by alternative ways of rearing sheep and this industry is eating away at natural lands because those numbers are far from natural. Even on a smaller scale, this system requires far more land than any plant-based, cellulosic or recycled fibre production system would.[19] Also, the methane gas released into our atmosphere when over a billion sheep pass, sheep breathe and belch has a devastating impact on our climate (small ruminants like sheep and goats are responsible for as many tonnes of carbon equivalent emissions as 103 million cars driving throughout a year, with cattle responsible for far more), and on the natural world we want to protect.[18]

Comparing annual small ruminant emissions to driving cars:

× 440,000

Land use comparison for one sweater:

Australian wool

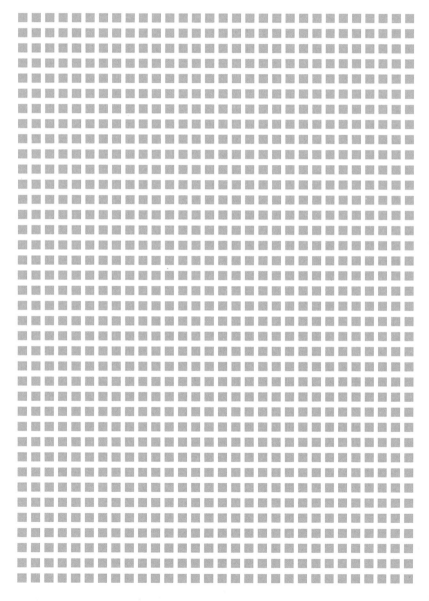

▦ – 1 m²

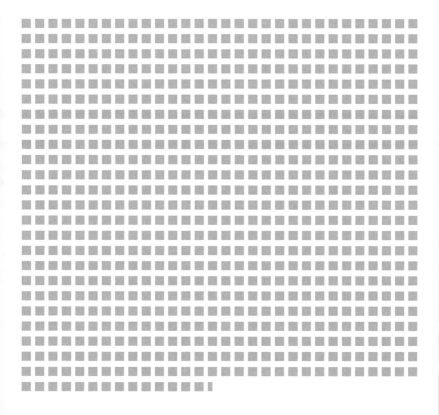

Australian cotton

Tencel lyocell

* Reference: Hakansson E. 'Fibre land use comparison', CIRCUMFAUNA, 2022 (verified by Faunalytics)

We need to be driven by real-life impact, not by senses of what's 'natural' or what seems sustainable. Human invention may not be 'natural' but it's long existed, evolved and helped the natural world, producing more land-efficient plant fibres, less resource-intensive dyes, and bio-materials which marry what's natural and what's invented perfectly for the benefit of the planet and us all.

While we need to move beyond inefficient and harmful material production, it's not only about fossil fuels and animal production systems. We've also got deforestation for irresponsible cellulosic materials, toxic pesticides in many conventional cotton fields, dyes which render biodegradable fibres no longer so, and a dauntingly long list of other woes to work out.[20-24]

When people are surveyed on what environmental factors matter when they make purchases, they often speak about things like sustainable and recycled materials, durability and a lack of hazardous chemicals used, but we don't really hear about degrowth.[24-27] We don't often hear about it because it's not something so easily sold or understood.

Degrowth

We keep viewing sustainability in fashion through a lens of 'looking after the environment in the way that is most in line with economic growth'. But that's a huge part of the problem because, among other factors, degrowth is a prerequisite to our ever being able to achieve 'sustainable fashion', and degrowth is about shrinking the fashion industry's scale.[28] It's about decoupling financial growth from fashionable success. In fact, some experts suggest that the industry must reduce in size fourfold in order to stay within planetary boundaries.[29] Perhaps not surprising when we've moved from a fashion industry with four weather-based seasons, to one with 52 micro-seasons; one for each week, if not more.[28]

How we view fashion and sustainability

Present
52 micro-seasons of clothing
(and far more of them)

Past
Four seasons of clothing
(and fewer of them)

Needed future
Fourfold decrease in extraction
and production

Present
Fashion industry extracting
and producing beyond
planetary boundaries

While these critical calls can't be ignored, 'shrinking' doesn't sound very appealing. Reframed, degrowth is about allowing more space for longevity, for repairing, for caring for clothes. Degrowth in fashion production means flourishing natural environments and cultural re-engagement with fashion as a kind of creativity and not only of consumerism. It means the development of fashion, the transformation of industry from one which is linear – always taking and always throwing away – into one which is circular, constantly reinventing and innovating, not just extracting.[30] A different, more nourishing kind of growth. Maybe we should talk about 'regrowth' in fashion.

The work of environmental science towards more sustainable fashion is complex, as it should be, working for our magnificently complex Earth. We are faced with a complicated mass of different but interconnected environmental considerations and, as a result, our solution is neither simple, individualistic nor singular. We can't leave saving the planet to citizen consumers and their purchases alone; rather it must be a whole ecosystem of people, brands and governments working collectively. There's no use seeking one specific, singular answer to how fashion can be more environmentally responsible, no fruitful quest for the thing-that-will-fix-everything-even-if-we-did-nothing-else. Instead, the golden solution is looking broadly, holistically.

We need to address the major emissions tied to the scale of fashion, to fossil fuel production, the rearing of ruminants for leather, wool and cashmere, and our industry's energy production all at once. But we also can't be locked into 'carbon tunnel vision', the dangerous way in which we sometimes strive for net-zero, for drastically reduced emissions, while ignoring biodiversity destruction, the polluting of soils, skies and seas, how poverty, inequality, racism, speciesism and classism contribute to our overarching environmental crisis.[31, 32] Essentially, we can't fall into the trap of seeing sustainability as some island of a thing, when everything on our planet touches, interweaves, alters the others.

We need degrowth. We need clean energy. We need to change the materials we use, and we need to work towards these all together and simultaneously, in a broad and diverse web of people dedicated to life on Earth.

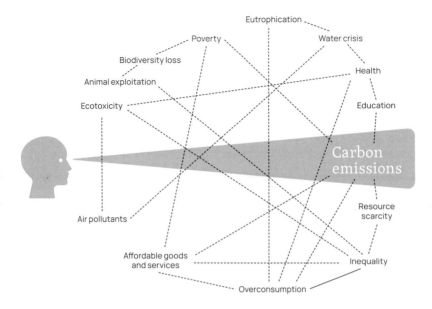

Eutrophication
Water crisis
Poverty
Biodiversity loss
Health
Animal exploitation
Ecotoxicity
Education
Carbon emissions
Air pollutants
Resource scarcity
Affordable goods and services
Inequality
Overconsumption

* Concept by Jan Konietzko, with new addition of animal exploitation

Ironically, much talk of sustainability and the environment lacks life. It lacks a connection to nature; to land, to insects, to animals, plants and fungi, to who we are – the kind of connection which Indigenous communities have fostered and which we have, at best, ignored and fractured and, at worst, decimated. This is being remedied now, in large part by a growing chorus of young, Indigenous, Black and Brown people (often women) who are refusing status quo discussions of the environment which do not look at the whole.[33] They recognise we don't just need lowered emissions and more protected lands: we need climate and environmental justice, the unpacking of environmental racism, neocolonialism, objectification of individuals and a western view of environmental abundance as nothing more than a richness of resources for profitable extraction.

The hyper-capitalistic, human-led fall of our natural world is not just a loss of resources, it's a loss of life. And when we talk about life, we have to talk about ethics.

4.
How we view fashion and ethics

'Ethical fashion' and 'sustainable fashion' are widely spoken of today as two separate entities, important but unrelated causes. However, the two intersect all the time: through environmental racism; the polluting of human communities who suffer related health consequences; through fashion's impediment of Indigenous land rights; and when the exploitation of individuals at once leads to environmental destruction.[1-3] While we view 'ethical fashion' as clothes made by people who are treated and paid fairly and 'sustainable fashion' as clothes made in a way which respects the planet and its boundaries, the two shouldn't be seen as parallel binaries which never blur together as one.

To begin our look into fashion and ethics, it makes sense to start with the people behind our clothes. In the wake of Rana Plaza's collapse in Bangladesh, Fashion Revolution got more people than ever before asking the question: 'Who made my clothes?'.

In 2013, the building, packed full of thousands of people sewing clothes for big-name, western, high-street brands, crumbled, crushing the people inside. The building had been declared unsafe and those people sewing inside had expressed fear for their lives before they were forced to continue working.[4]

1,134 people were killed, another 2,600 were injured. The unimaginable tragedy of this event caught the world's attention and, for the first time, spotlighted those we'd never really seen or thought of, but whose skillful work we wear every day.[4, 5]

As many as 80% of garment working people are women of colour.[6] Brands continue to pay these women very little so that they can make a lot, contributing to global inequality and poverty, while allowing for discrimination and violence in garment factories.[5] It can be hard to picture the suffering behind a single shirt, dress or pair of pants. Those with lived experience of this suffering are intentionally kept from our view to maintain our comfortable ignorance. Kunthear Mov, who co-founded ethical brand Dorsu after working in a sweatshop herself, changed that for me.

'On a normal day we had to wake up
early in the morning, at about 5:30am,
to arrive before the bell rings at 7am
when we start working.

We were meant to finish work at 4pm but most
of the time we were forced to work until 9pm.
If you didn't have enough materials and made
a request to complete your sewing, the
managers would yell. There was no room for
mistakes. They yelled at people most days: if not
at me, at the other people around me.

We were not allowed to talk, have any jokes
with each other, or have fun, we just had to keep
working, working, working. I got to do one thing,
finishing zippers, over and over for months at
a time, you never get a chance to do anything
else. If people brought their lunch into work,
they had no space to sit and eat properly so they
would find somewhere to sit on the ground near
the wall. To me, it just looked like there was no
value in people like us.

We couldn't have toilet breaks when
we needed to, we had to take turns using
tickets and someone would record the time
we were gone and when we came back.

→

If we asked for a day off, for whatever reason,
it's not just that you wouldn't get paid
but you would also have the manager yelling
at you. So you couldn't get sick. We worked
six days a week, but also, they would still force
us to work on Sundays.

I wish people would want to know
where their clothes come from,
and to try and not just want cheap things
without minding where they are made.
If they want the cost of clothes to get lower
they force us to be the machines.

Now, I feel like I am a person with my own voice,
a person of value, and I am proud of my work
and that our business is good for the community.
At my old factory job, they looked down
on us. When I talk about it I feel so emotional,
and it's hard to get away the feeling
that I don't have value or was unvalued
and mistreated. I just would like to see factories
at least make us feel like we are a person
equal to any person. You really see clearly
if you are in that situation that you are not valuable,
you are hardly a person. That feels really hard.'

— Kunthear Mov,
   who worked in a sweatshop before co-founding ethical brand Dorsu

It was Kunthear's story and wisdom which first made me think about how clothes impact lives, when I was 15 and in Cambodia. Having bought a t-shirt which probably came from a factory like the one she had spoken about earlier that week, meeting her brought my choices and their direct impacts right up to my face, hot and sweaty.

This kind of exploitation occurs across the supply chain, not only at tier one. Children forced to collect mulberry leaves to feed silkworms while women burn their hands boiling the cocoons;[7] people made to pick cotton from plants, spraying fields with carcinogenic pesticides and looming the fibres into fabrics for next to no pay;[8] those working in the back-breaking work of shearing without access to safe equipment and fair remuneration, let alone a toilet;[9] and those roughly combing goats for meagre monetary gain as they watch their degrading grasslands disappear.[10] It's in these parts of fashion where exploitation and modern slavery get wrapped up with our environmental crises.

An estimated 40.2 million enslaved people today are forced to contribute to disproportionate environmental destruction and greenhouse gas emissions.[11] If the work of modern slavery were a country, it would be the third largest CO_2 emitter in the world, after China and the United States.[11] This perpetuates a vicious cycle, as this contribution to rising pollutants and temperatures impacts human life again, creating the kinds of vulnerability and displacement which put people at risk of entrapment within modern slavery to begin with.[11] Much of this slavery is tied up in deforestation, which we know in turn impacts global emissions, biodiversity, wildlife and many Indigenous peoples in and around many leather supply chains, as well as in cellulosic supply chains producing viscose and rayon.[3, 11-14]

This expanded view is already broader than the mainstreamed version of ethical fashion pushed out today. But there's more: these supply chains also include animals. There's the wildlife who are endangered by deforestation, like great gliders, swift parrots, jaguars, giant otters, spot-tailed quolls, koalas, toucans and tapirs across some global leather supply chains.[15] There are those species threatened by inefficient land use, our warming climate and pollution.[16] And, finally, those largely invisible within the conversation of 'ethical fashion', the animals whose exploitation is at the core of so much material production: the animals whose wool, hair, fur, feathers and skins we've come to consider mere materials for our wearing.

As many as 1.5 billion animals are skinned in fashion supply chains for leather each year, and at least one hundred million more for their fur-filled skins.[17-19] The weight of our moral responsibility to so many individuals in fashion is so heavy a burden that many of us simply choose to ignore it. Perhaps ignoring it feels easier and less confronting – whether it's acceptable is another thing.

Animals skinned in fashion supply chains

× 3,750,000

Ethics relate to moral principles. Those who ought to be offered moral consideration are, simply, all those whose wellbeing would benefit from such consideration. We give (or should give, or pretend to give) other people moral consideration because we know they, like us, think and feel. How we treat them and the morality of that treatment directly impacts that individual, their quality of life, whether they suffer, whether they live or die. The same is true for the animals of fashion, like ducks, cows, goats, sheep, snakes, crocodiles, foxes, minks, alpacas, kangaroos, ostriches and so many others.[20]

The Cambridge Declaration on Consciousness recognises that 'the absence of a neocortex does not appear to preclude an organism from experiencing affective states... non-human animals have the neuroanatomical, neurochemical, and neurophysiological substrates of conscious states along with the capacity to exhibit intentional behaviours. Consequently, the weight of evidence indicates that humans are not unique in possessing the neurological substrates that generate consciousness.'[21] No surprise to anyone who has ever spent any time with anyone of any other species, this was the very official and academic way of stating what is no longer of any reasonable scientific debate: animals are conscious, feeling individuals like us. They feel joy, comfort, pain and fear just as we do. In fashion, pain and fear are far more prevalent.

Despite this acknowledgement, we shy away from acting on that pain and fear. There are some exceptions. Most of us agree on one ethical issue in fashion: that the fur industry is abhorrent, because it's unacceptable to kill animals specifically for clothing, just as Donatella Versace said ("I don't want to kill animals to make fashion").[22] While the fur industry persists and continues to confine and kill wild animals each year, demand and legal acceptability of the trade is ever shrinking. We're moving towards a more general consensus of the same kind as relating to reptiles skinned for the wealthiest few. But our feelings on cows, sheep and other animals in fashion tend to be more complicated.

What's said in defence of wearing animals

It's argued that wearing the skin of a cow is different from wearing the skin of a raccoon dog because the cow is also and already being killed for consumption. This premise is wrapped up in the notion of leather as a by-product; a notion which is false, given skins are such valuable co-products that the industry is worth hundreds of billions of dollars, and more profitable skin sales means more cows are bred.[23] The distinction between cow and raccoon dog, leather and fur, one skin and another skin is also one of speciesism: discrimination based on species.

We've been culturally conditioned to view some species as more worthy of moral consideration, similarly to the way in which we're conditioned to feel the same about some genders and races – perhaps the reason most exploited garment workers are women of colour.

The decision to offer one gender, race or species more safeties than another is arbitrary,[24] but it's why our fashion system is the way it is. Exploitation exported to poorer, darker-skinned nations, women bearing the brunt of fashion's pain, and animals so abstracted through exploitation that we don't really see them at all.

We more easily justify wearing the skins of certain animals because we've inherited a system designed to allow us to do so.[25] This is true even linguistically, and we know language is powerful: it's why fashion's advertisements can so effectively green-wash and ethics-wash profitable harm. Language allows for cognitive dissonance – where we uncomfortably hold conflicting beliefs – and for distance.[25] Distance from things like who made our clothes, from the reality of 'leather' as skin, and from how we actually believe others should be treated. If it didn't, we wouldn't all be buying, designing and selling clothes we'd hate to see produced.

This distance – set up not only through language, but visually – means when we pull on the calf skin boots we don't think of who stitched them, who bathed the skin in chromium, who held the knife, or what they saw when that skin was pulled off the hot, wet carcass of a young calf who was sawn open after. We think of the glossy advertisement of the pretty model wearing them while standing amongst the flowers, and of the 'responsible' label they've been given. We don't even begin to imagine how that calf's entrails sounded slapping onto a blood-caked floor to be thrown out, the smell wafting over those who live nearby. Cows can sense distress through smell, and do so in slaughterhouses full of nervous urine, dripping red knives and wide-eyed, panicked animals.[23]

What fashion hides and shows us

But fashion doesn't like to talk about this. It doesn't like to acknowledge any of this as an issue to overcome and it certainly doesn't want to attach discussion of this exploitation to ethics. That's not very sexy. So, the most common way animals are considered and spoken of in fashion is through a smaller and more palatable definition, one often lumped in with sustainability – as though animals are a part of the unthinking and unconscious parts of our planet, like fossil fuels themselves. Mainstream fashion talks about 'welfare', it doesn't talk about 'rights' – fashion thinks those who do are extremists – so instead fashion talks about how it can continue to take from animals, so long as fashion minimises distress while doing so. Fashion glazes over the part where fashion ultimately takes animals' lives without need, and over the ethics of viewing individuals as 'stock', as commodities to profit from through cutting, plucking and killing.

Certification, commodification and consent

Almost all of fashion's animal welfare schemes and certifications are filled with gaping holes. A Responsible Wool Standard which still permits the tails of lambs to be cut off without pain relief, in some instances.[26] A Responsible Down Standard which offers the cramped factory-farming of ducks slaughtered before plucking as a 'humane' alternative to plucking them first, killing them later.[27, 28] A Leather Working Group certification which actually does refer to what's 'ethical', despite offering their seal of approval to brands with not even so much as an awareness of where – let alone how – animals whose skins they sell were raised or slaughtered.[29] Currently, fashion is a system where unnecessary and fought against death is unquestioned, but prettied up for sale.

If fashion's talk of 'fair wages' to hide the fact that 'living wages' are not being paid is misleading (the former is generally not legally defined, so it's easy to promise without doing anything),[30] fashion's reference to 'animal welfare' in systems which profit from the mutilation and slaughter of those individuals is egregiously so.

The rights we want for fashion's working people, those which are so sorely needed from cotton fields to garment factories, are built around an understanding of bodily autonomy and of consent. We believe those in fashion should be free to consent and refuse, be free from exploitation, from harassment and from harm. A safe, autonomous, fair fashion industry, free from coercion, should be a core value in work towards genuinely ethical production. While so many humans do not work in such a fashion industry, animals in fashion's supply chains are offered no autonomy over their bodies, no capacity to consent to what they clearly would not. Their bodies are seen as resources to take from. Their willingness to live and be safe is routinely ignored and even reprimanded. Every industry which brings animals into the world for the purpose of production has guides which tell workers how to hold them down, restrain them, respond when they fight back.[23, 31–33] How to breed the fiercest out of existence, keeping only those most malleable to our will alive until the date we decide they won't be any longer. [34–36]

When we speak about welfare in relation to fashion's use of animals, we are talking about incremental change which lessens the amount of pain and suffering faced by an individual who does not own their own life. We're never talking about the core values of a right to consent and have autonomy over our bodies – the realm of welfare, of acceptable objectification, approved slaughter and dominion is out of alignment with these values, and inherently so. While 'welfare' talk is easier, it's failing to address that the wellbeing of an individual can't be genuinely considered so long as their life is given no more value than what money can be made from it.

No worker, no animal, no one should exist merely for profit extraction.

The way we view fashion and ethics today is dislocated from how we really view ethics. I know feminists, I know child protection advocates, I know people who work in the realm of body safety. I don't spend time with anyone who doesn't believe in the right to autonomous action, to safety and freedom from harm as concepts. I know plenty of people who talk about these issues while wearing clothes made by people and from animals who are denied these rights. It's what our current fashion system encourages, and deceives, us to do so.

The fashion industry has designed itself to make sure we avoid getting to the crux of what's wrong with it. If we did, we would move beyond viewing animals as materials, move beyond viewing people as machines to make clothes, and the planet as just a resource to profitably plunder. But, for now at least, fashion thinks that's too hard. Fashion would prefer to perpetuate the compounding deindividualisation and destruction of those in its supply chains, strengthening the fallacy of its acceptability in doing so, allowing us to, often unwittingly, conspire with the status quo.

But since when was good, interesting, beautiful and clever fashion ever about following the status quo or about being unthinking?

5.
Sustaining injustice

To recognise ethics and sustainability in fashion as one and the same is to define sustainability not only as what we can afford to continue with, but what we deem acceptable to. It is not only what we can literally sustain without pushing our planet's ecological boundaries (which, when crossed, risks abrupt and devastating environmental changes), but what is right to sustain. We may be able to sustain a fashion industry which exploits people who make clothes and farm fibres if we did so on a smaller scale, but it wouldn't be right to do so. While we cannot environmentally sustain the wool or down industry in its current scale, we may be able to sustain a version of these industries some very significant order of magnitudes smaller. But if we're still sustaining systems which kill those who are no longer profitable, or which must kill to function, why would the planetary sustainability of these industries be a good thing? In this sense, sustainability is about what and who we view as expendable, a worthwhile cost of clothing, whether that cost be the life of a grassland ecosystem, of a woman who spends almost all her waking hours sewing for a few dollars, or an animal whose being alive is not compatible with fashion's process of belt-making.

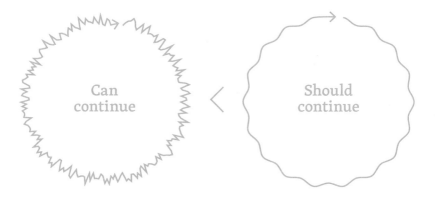

We cannot sustain destruction and objectification, a denial of life and of choice. Whether we are destroying the life and wellbeing of a river flowing along a dyehouse, feedlot or tannery, the life and wellbeing of a person denied bathroom breaks while sewing, or that of a sheep pinned down for shearing in the same way as they were restrained for painful castration, the core is the same.[1-3] These are injustices, different branches from the same root, and we cannot persist with creating fashion this way.

> When we think
> of what we can sustain,
> of what we want our
> fashion system to be like,
> we should work from
> our core values outward,
> and accept only what aligns
> with them: regeneration
> over destruction,
> honour and freedom
> over objectification,
> autonomy over dominion
> and mindful creativity
> over mass consumerism.

Ecofascism and a singular view of sustainability

Acknowledging the intersections between protecting our planet, those we share it with, and those of our same human species also serves to eliminate the potential for eco-fascism in fashion.[4] It helps to dismantle skewed views of environmentalism where to protect our Earth is presented as a justifiable reason to oppress, exploit, deny protection to and even kill individuals. This is the kind of threatening thinking which says that there are too many people on the planet to clothe, and so we need fewer people (and in the worst cases, to reduce populations through racially charged, violent means).[5] What we really need is for our western, capitalistic culture to stop pushing each person to buy a mountain's worth of clothes each year.

Explored through the lens of speciesism, ecofascism is the kind of thinking that justifies confining native crocodiles to cages legally shorter than the length of their own bodies, supposedly for the sake of 'population conservation', but really for luxury fashion's commercial gain upon slaughter and skinning, when ecotourism, public education and environmental restoration could do the trick.[6-7] Today, more native saltwater crocodiles in Australia live in factory-farms like those owned by and supplying the likes of Hermes and Louis Vuitton than live in their natural habitat: that's not any real kind of environmentalism.[7]

Environmental justice

Changing fashion so that we sustain neither environmental degradation nor injustice would be difficult if these two goals didn't align. But they do and often. We see racial injustices when Global Majority communities bear the brunt of pollution from fossil fuel mines, slaughterhouses and other damaging parts of fashion supply chains.[8-10] We know from peer-reviewed research that abolishing slavery would be one of the most effective methods of climate change mitigation,[11] and that simply paying living wages could cut back fashion's harmful environmental excess.[12] We know that people farming plant fibres in more responsibly managed systems are healthier, as are their communities.[13-15] That moving beyond the use of animal-derived materials could contribute to the freeing up of about 3 billion hectares of land for rewilding,[16] all the while sequestering greenhouse gases up to the past 16 years worth of all fossil fuel emissions, and drastically slashing methane (as the IPCC demands), if we did it by 2050.[17] The transition will be complex, but the ways in which our problems interweave actually help to make it easier.

●

Changing our understanding of sustainability to look beyond what can be sustained to what should be sustained – in a way which results in meaningful change – will be hard work. Understanding the solutions is, of course, as critical as understanding the problems. In our efforts to build a roadmap towards a cultural, legislative and industrial revolution which supports fashion that prioritises life before profit, we consistently hit a roadblock – our societal eagerness to sustain ever-growing profits at the price of everything else.

> It's our idea that money, rather than wellbeing, clean air, functioning ecosystems, and a lack of bloodshed, violence and exploitation, makes us rich.

Is this the sort of argument that gets shunned as unrealistic and uneducated, especially if it is made by a person of colour, or an Indigenous person? Yes. Should it be? No.

There are alternatives to infinite growth capitalism and a fashion industry which spins out of control under it. Whole countries are moving to measure their success outside of Gross Domestic Product (GDP), looking at wellbeing over finance.[18, 19] Bhutan is a wonderful example, one which prioritises its 'Gross National Happiness Index' and ignores calls by the World Bank to 'utilise' its pristine old-growth forests, instead valuing them for all they are while standing.[20, 21] The city of Amsterdam has embraced doughnut economics, which aims to ensure both a social foundation to protect individuals, and an ecological ceiling to protect the planet.[22, 23] Marketplaces where, as Professor Esther Leslie puts it, lots of individual makers create 'not to stay alive, to make money out of others' incompetence, but in order to showcase their abilities [and] their ideas', exist now, putting expression first.[24] These alternatives have already been thought up, and they are already working in the small spaces where they've been accepted or allowed to remain.

6.
Total ethics fashion explained

If we're working to sustain a system which honours what lives,
and which does not accept destruction and oppression, we are working
for a 'total ethics fashion' system. Given language's power over our systems
and lives, it's important this system be named, especially when so many other terms
exist and have fallen short of their goal.

The term 'total ethics fashion' exists to express intersections and collectivity
where other concepts and terms related to responsible production, consumption
and relationships with fashion have not. It exists to demand an all-encompassing
and holistic view of this responsibility, and of care. To counter the increasing
narrowness of terms like 'ethical fashion', 'fair fashion', 'vegan fashion', 'sustainable
fashion', 'cruelty-free fashion' and 'eco-friendly fashion', which have been overused
and misused to such a degree the meaning is twisted, contorted and eventually lost.

The vision that these terms represent are important – who wouldn't want a fair,
sustainable and cruelty-free fashion industry? – but they've been transformed
into marketing terms, sometimes used disingenuously, other times with the best
of intentions, but in ways that don't quite make sense or represent the true values
these words ought to hold.[1]

We see advertisements for 'sustainable' clothes that may use less
environmentally impactful materials, but which are produced at such a rapid
pace that they sustain an extractive, polluting system far out of alignment
with environmental protection. These types of misleading marketing claims take
advantage of public goodwill.

But even if these clothes were indeed made slowly – in line with the values
of a system which produced less, encouraged the care and repair of clothes,
the recreation of them into something new when they were no longer
worn – 'sustainable' may still not be the right word for them. This is true
when we remember that our idea of what is 'sustainable fashion' is based on our idea
of what can acceptably be sustained, and for now, these ideas keep forgetting
the plight of the individuals within our Earthly environment, who are a part of nature.

'Sustainable' fashion which is not made ethically is not sustainable. Yet, we see
this 'sustainable' label slapped onto garments made by people paid so little
they struggle to sustain themselves and their families. We're promised
'sustainability' while buying garments made from the skins, feathers and hair
of animals who have been denied their right to sustain life itself.

Just as our view of what can be sustained needs to be expanded, our understanding of what justifies labels like 'ethical' and 'fair' being touted by brands selling things like bags and sweaters needs to broaden. When these labels proudly note the living wages paid to those who stitched and knitted them, but overlook the people further back in those supply chains, as well as animals themselves, we aren't viewing ethics in its totality. There's nothing ethical about public health being harmed by wool scouring pollution,[2] or about the industry standard practice of slaughtering sheep when their wool production slows and they're no longer profitable.[3] Fairness doesn't deserve to be placed near a supply chain which forcibly removes Indigenous communities from the forests they protect and belong to,[4] or which makes shoes from individuals who struggled for their lives in an impossibly imbalanced fight.[5]

Similarly, 'vegan' and 'cruelty-free' labels in fashion too often forget about the callously cruel treatment of children forced to work on cotton farms,[6] of people whose babies lie at their feet, listening to the whirring of sewing machines from dawn until dark as their mothers work to afford to feed their families. Not one product made through these processes gives the deserved moral consideration to everyone involved. Not one ought to exist unchanged in our future total ethics fashion system.

When these terms and promises are used and made inconsistently, they lose their original meanings, the ones that existed before 'fashion' was tacked onto the end of them. 'Total ethics fashion' seeks to collect up what's been lost, to secure those meanings as essential to its definition.

Total ethics fashion also seeks to demand specificity over other terms and words, too. To set a higher standard than that which the fashion industry currently accepts. Fashion uses 'regenerative', not only to speak to the regrowth of a tarnished planetary system, but unfortunately too, for promoting products which eat away at natural lands through inefficiency, and which are built upon animal exploitation and slaughter.[5, 7] We use words like 'responsible' but without demanding they reflect consistent responsibility towards all life and its protection, rather than just some processes. Language develops naturally over time, but not always in a way that is useful or accurate. Total ethics fashion aims to counter this unhelpful language progression (or perhaps more aptly, regression) by becoming more specific, intentional and all-encompassing.

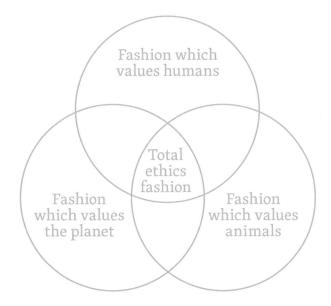

The concept of total ethics fashion is as simple as it is vast: the life and wellbeing of the planet and all those who live here – us humans and the other animals here alongside us – must be prioritised before profit and production.
Total ethics fashion doesn't accept the protection of some at the expense of others, or a barren definition of environmental protection which claims to preserve the life of the environment, and yet not the lives of those on this planet, who are a part of this environment, be they human or non-human. It recognises that if we do not address harm and destruction in fashion holistically, we will never be rid of harm and destruction. It refuses binary or only partially collective thinking, advocacy and efforts. A dedication to total ethics fashion means a dedication to a genuinely holistic, full approach to fashion and to justice.

Put more simply, total ethics fashion is the convergence of care for the life of the planet and all those who live on it, too.

This is not to say efforts on behalf of one of these groups alone are not important: they are, and deeply so. But while work to protect the planet, people and animals from fashion's destructive ways is noble and progresses fashion forward by some metrics, such isolated works too often allow the perpetuation of the root causes of the harm we want to weed out.

When we promote belts made by those paid living wages but which are made with an animal's skin, we confuse and so weaken what we may think of as a symbolic example of fashion made with respect for autonomy, consent and freedom. When we push the fast sale of purses made from synthetic, petrochemical PVC while sticking a green leaf-embellished 'vegan' swing tag, we blur and fall short of promises to value life on Earth.

Consistency is core to total ethics fashion, because it's with consistency that we are able to become more clear about why we should create fashion in a certain way, about why we hold the values we do, create and dress as we do. Without this consistency, we let water in the boat of our sense of responsibility in fashion, and we start sinking into a sea of green-washing and ethics-washing.

7.
Humans
as animals

Presenting total ethics fashion as the convergence of care between three different groups which intersect still isn't really accurate either (though it's what I just did). We have to go further. Two of the circles need to become one, because though we tend to forget it, humans are animals too.

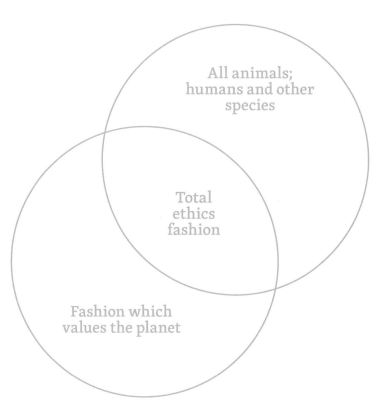

Humans are just 0.01% of all life on Earth, and just 2.5% of animal biomass.[1] Remembering this boggles the mind and helps us to realise that while we've built a system which puts us above everyone else (with a clear and oppressive hierarchy amongst us humans, too), we're a part of a much larger and intricate web of life. The similarities between us and our fellow species on this Animalia branch of life are far greater than our differences. While we know scientifically that those who share animality with us also share sentience, our framing of other animals in society as things here for our use obscures what this really means.

> When it comes
> to what should count,
> when it comes to pain
> and a desperate
> will for freedom from it,
> we're all nakedly the same.

For those animals tied up in our fashion system, our similarities rooted in sentience include our excitement in learning new things (cows skinned for leather),[2] our recognition and relation to different emotions on the faces of others (sheep shorn for wool and skinned for leather),[3] and our hearing of hurting and happiness in each other's voices (goats combed for cashmere then skinned for leather).[4] We share rich emotional lives – and I emphasise emotion, because intelligence should never be the defining factor between who is treated well and who is abused, in any part of our society.[5]

Yet one way we humans do differ from other animals is in our capacity for moral reasoning that can initiate changed behaviour at a broad, societal level. While other animals hold 'moral emotions' like sympathy and patience, some acting altruistically – even when it has come at a loss to them – they are not 'moral agents'.[6] Put simply, this means scientists think that other animals lack the conceptual, cognitive abilities that mean they should be held accountable for their behaviours to the same degree as human animals. A mink doesn't have the capacity to consider the ethics of their fish hunting or to then change their behaviour, but our greater moral capacity means we can and must consider the ethics of confining such minks to cages, and gassing them for coats and keyrings. This distinction between us and other animals like us is important because it offers us choice, including the choice to opt out of needless harm, and the choice to deconstruct our view of humans as entirely separate from the animal kingdom we continue to evolve inside of.

Dehumanisation and oppression

To deconstruct the idea of 'human' may seem like 'dehumanisation',
and this can seem disturbing because we think of dehumanisation as a bad, corrupt
process. But that's only because those who are viewed as other than human
are viewed as less than human, and so viewed as acceptably harmed.

Nasreen Sheik, the founder of Empowerment Collective, said:

'I became a textile worker
when I was 9 or 10 years
old. We were forced
to work from 6 am
to 11 pm You don't feel
human… We ate,
we slept and we worked
in that sweatshop.
The room itself literally
looked like a prison cell…
if we were so lucky,
and we did all the work
on time, they would give
us rotten grapes.

> So I tell people
> that we were literally fed
> like animals and forced
> to work like machines.'[7]

In *The Pedagogy of the Oppressed*, Paulo Freire wrote that 'concern for humanisation leads at once to the recognition of dehumanisation'.[8] Meanwhile, Christopher Sebastian notes that it was 'actually white supremacy that set up human as a political identity', manifesting the view that some people – those who aren't white and who aren't men – should be seen as less human and more animal, justifying their ongoing oppression.[9] So long as we see that some other animals can be harmed for fashion, we will also see that some humans can be harmed for fashion.

If we seek to create a fashion industry which is free from oppression and which genuinely recognises individual rights, safeties and autonomies, we need a fashion industry which sees that humans are animals who must not be harmed, just as with any other animal. This consistency, this equalisation, leaves no room for hierarchy, no room for punching down, or for justifying harm. It lays bare all exploitation for exactly what it is, and asks simply for fashion to view that exploitation as something to avoid, navigate around and move past without exception.

Oppressive system

Humans viewed
as complete
(e.g. white men)

Humans deemed
less human
(e.g. people of colour)

Animals other than humans
deemed more valuable
(e.g. minks, dogs)

Animals other
than humans
(e.g. cows)

Just system

All animals regardless of species
or other diverse factors

A total ethics fashion
system must be one
free from violence:
the violence of denied
consent, denied safety,
of neglect, and of physical,
knife-wielding violence.
Picking and choosing which
kinds and directions of harm
can be justified and dressed
up in meaningless fashion
policy speak means failing
to see the connections
between violences in fashion.

If we expect all people working to create garments, shoes
and accessories to have safe, dignified work, all along the supply chain,
what do we do with slaughterhouse workers in those supply chains? This work is left
to society's most vulnerable because no one wants to do it, and while it's poorly
paying, physically dangerous work, that's not the half of it.[10] Some of the symptoms
faced by those traumatised by their inherently violent work include 'drug and alcohol
abuse, anxiety, panic, depression, increased paranoia, a sense of disintegration,
dissociation or amnesia', similarly faced by soldiers who have slaughtered other

people in war.[10] People often faint on their first tour of their new abattoir workplace and the spots are so hard to fill refugees have been offered express visas if they'll do the work.[11, 12] While 'emotions in the abattoir tended to be bottled up' despite the distress the work causes, as one worker noted, those emotions change us all the same, changing how we view others, and we see this in fashion.[13]

'If compassion were a muscle, this work we did left it weak and atrophied', said Susana Chavez, after leaving her slaughterhouse work.[14]

Our acceptance of skins and feathers from these slaughterhouses, used as materials, weakens our industry's and our culture's capacity for compassion too, no matter who it is extended to. If we can justify dressing up in and profiting from someone being killed, we can justify anything – we can certainly justify paying people poorly.

Fashion plays such a significant role in culture creation and evolution. It's never been just about the threads that make up fabrics which in turn make up clothes: it's always been about the ideas and expressions they represent about their makers and wearers, and who we want to be.

Fashion's celebration
of our animality
could be both a playground
for art and innovation,
while also a tool
for the just and responsible
reconstruction of its supply
chains: creating them flat,
not from top to bottom
where some profit, others
are impoverished, and others
are degraded, shackled,
denied a life worth living
or a life at all.

8.
Animals as nature

I'm merging the circles again, though for the last time, because now there's just one.
Because if humans are animals, animals are nature. Protecting the planet
isn't something that has a secondary benefit to us: it is protecting us.

Total
ethics
fashion
(Fashion which values
nature, values life)

The oceans full of microfibres are like the waters that we're made of, and that now
also have microplastics in them.[1, 2] The burning of forests see tree rings, which mirror
our fingerprints, burned to ash. The destruction of natural environments matter
because life matters, because suffering matters, and the wellbeing of all life on Earth
is reliant on that wellbeing being collective.[3] If shedding 'humanity' to recognise
'animality' protects us all as individuals, seeing us all as a part of nature rather
than as simply living amongst it protects all life on this pale blue dot. But our current
fashion system, and in fact the legal system it sits under, does not see us this way.

Legal personhood and what gets protection

Today, legal personhood is offered only to humans almost all of the time.[4]
Legal personhood is the only way for someone or something to be recognised by law
as the subject of rights and duties, and it is what gives us privileges and protections
that cannot (in theory) be taken away from us. Someone forced to pick cotton in Xinjiang
has their rights violated.[2] This injustice sits within a legal framework where this person
is recognised as having rights, making it a little easier to fight for those rights
to be upheld. Justice for other animals in fashion is more difficult because in our legal
system, and so in our cultural system, they are property. Someone who rescues a fox
from a fur farm's wire cage before they are electrocuted is charged with property theft.
Animals beyond the human species are considered legal things, live stock,
which can be owned like coat hangers or shirts, and as a result, laws which aim
to protect them are more easily knocked down by those who own them.[6]

Similarly, natural entities are things not persons. It's why ecocide by fast fashion giants
is so difficult to address legally, why regulations try and often fail to protect trees
from being cut down and waterways from being coloured by dyes and fashion production
wastes: the environment has no legal right to its existence. This is true in almost
all cases, aside from in some remarkable wins, such as when the Indigenous Maori people
of Aotearoa (New Zealand) secured legal personhood to the Te Awa Tupua river.[7] Te Awa
Tupua now has rights that trump human and business-driven will which could destroy it.

While animals beyond the human species and environments we live as part
of are denied rights, large corporations are afforded legal personhood all the time.[8]
Companies become juridical persons so that they can be independent from the people
who create them, to protect the finances of those people should anything go wrong
– including should a business be sued for huge sums of money, even as compensation
for violating human rights, for systemic violence against other animals, or for massive
environmental destruction.[9] It also protects companies from investigation
without warrant, and from other things which legal persons are protected from:
even when this business protection means harm to living persons.

The way that our legal system prioritises corporations over life is exploited
by the fashion industry. H&M, Inditex which owns Zara, SHEIN and every other
major fashion brand which produce endless amounts of clothes, which fill landfills,
use dangerous chemicals, kill our fellow animals, degrade land and contribute
to the climate crisis all have legal personhood. It's how business structures are set
up under law. Those animals and environments they exploit do not. Those who make

their clothes do, but their power to exercise their legal personhood is unmatched by the power of corporate judicial personhood.

If we recognise ourselves as part of nature, and so our creations, our fashion as also a part of nature, we see just how wrong this all is, and how in the long run, how it does no one any good. In academic parlance, this would be referred to as moving from an anthropocentric value system to one that's eco-centric,[10] which is critical to achieving genuine sustainability. Eco-centric values have been carried through generations of Indigenous communities, as kinds of ancient wisdom – including in places where fashion and industry now ravage Indigenous lands.[11] On the lands now called Australia where Aboriginal people fight against expanding sheep and cattle ranching, alongside fossil fuel mining, and in Amazonia, where similar fights against deforestation and pollution persist.

We're more likely to protect the planet if we hold biospheric rather than egoistic values – when we judge something based on how it impacts the world around us rather than our individual own resources, power or achievement.[12–14]

But what if we could dissolve singular, self-serving motivations in fashion, and in culture, by leaning into our intimacy and oneness with nature, in a way which western societies have forgotten?[15]

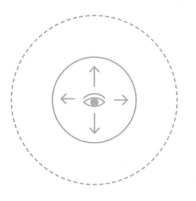

Egoistic
view

Biospheric
view

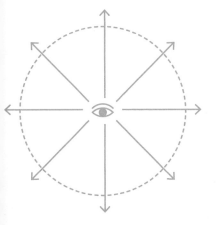

Eco-centric
view

What would fashion look like if we saw us as a whole, if the degradation of a garment-working person hurt like our own degradation, hurt like the air being choked by smoke from flaming piles of discarded clothes, hurt like the degradation of grasslands roamed by commodified calves, hurt like the spilling blood as those calves became carry bags? Where would we be? We could ask what we'd be left with, what else we could take, but in the abundance of a world where we genuinely valued the planet we exist as part of, which we create clothing within, the question is what more, what better could we create?

Creation flourishes when nature is put first. We've seen that the leaves of pineapple plants grown by people in the Philippines can be saved from burning and, instead, made into a material to be used in the place of skins.[16] We've discovered the expansiveness of natural, bio-based substances, stretching the fashion industry past fossil-fuel derived elastane.[17] We're seeing that nature has what we need without looting it, especially when we get creative.

Our environment, our fellow
sentient beings, ourselves
and our collective health
cannot be unwoven.
When we prioritise profit
and production over any
one of these, we fail us all.
We also fail the creative art
and potential of fashion,
which cannot exist
on a decimated Earth,
where we cannot exist
to create.

9.
Designing supply chains as we design clothing and outfits

Not all clothes are made or designed well. Many are ripped off from smaller designers by fast fashion giants with no time for creativity, sewn by people who are not afforded time to stitch them with the care and skill they possess. Good fashion takes thought and time. It takes looking outward for inspiration, a keen eye, a patience which allows not for the newness of constant manufacturing, but a newness of ideas. We need to get back to that patient practice. We also need to go further.

The amount of attention and care we give to our clothing, to the way a fabric falls, the perfect width of a strap, the right amount of pattern clashing, the balance of elegance and effortlessness, the minute details of a collar, the most perfect stitching, is what makes fashion an artform. Considered, detailed, playful, personal. This same level of scrutiny and interest needs to be given to fashion supply chains, too, so that the beauty the wearer sees is equal to the beauty of fashion's process of creation. If the fashion industry put as much energy into designing supply chains that respect our natural world, us all, as it put into designing and making beautiful garments, we'd have a more beautiful world for those garments to exist in.

It shouldn't be an added bonus that something is physically made and not just designed with care: it should be the bare minimum, the least we will accept from fashion. While it's more challenging to think of a new business model which isn't reliant on infinite growth on a finite planet, which doesn't deem human and other animals as production units, old-growth forests as feedstocks and rivers as garbage disposals, that's what we have to do together. If the many minds behind garments are not great enough to collectively ensure their entire creation is considered – from the field where a plant grows to the folded-up garment being taken home by its new, adoring owner – those minds are not equipped to be in fashion.

We must recognise that the fashion industry does not only design clothes, it designs supply chains, and in turn, it designs environments. When we buy clothes, we curate not only our wardrobes and our outfits, but we curate landscapes and biomes. We decide if the planet will be stripped bare of biodiversity, of life and of wellbeing, or if we will allow it to be cloaked in a rich abundance of floral and faunal life.

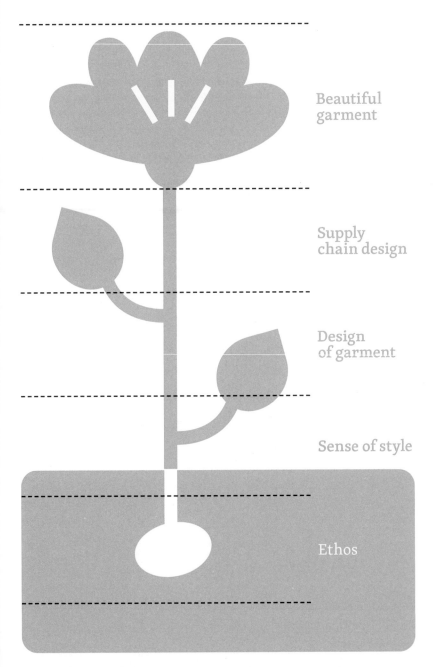

Beautiful
garment

Supply
chain design

Design
of garment

Sense of style

Ethos

More personally, through fashion we also create and display our ethos.
We show what we accept and celebrate, and what we do not. The common thread
between fashion's modern slavery, the mutilation and killing of animals,
and the wrecking of our natural environment and those who belong to it is a denial
of autonomy rooted in the idea that some lives are more precious than others.
It is the acceptance of commodifying individuals to cogs in a machine, to mere
materials, to simple resources here only to profit from. We may not have ever
thought about this before, but once we have, we can choose not to dress up in that.
We can sew with a more ethically robust kind of thread.

Deciding what sort
of ethos we want to robe
ourselves in and design
with helps us to better
imagine innovative paths
forward to a fashion
system which encapsulates
these values.

10.
Innovation and a just transition

A conceptual total ethics fashion system is inevitably complicated by the nitty gritty details of a transition towards a real system. This kind of transition is complex, geopolitical, often expensive and hard. There's no questioning that. But we've changed for the better before: many forms of child labour have now been outlawed,[1] making it far less common (though still a persistent problem in some fashion supply chains); human innovation will soon see the total repair of the ozone's hole;[2] I could go on – and we will again. And too, on talks of costs, the climate crisis, global pandemics, species extinction and exploitation are also costs. Steep ones. As noted by Waorani woman and leader Nemonte Nenquimo, these are driven by 'widespread spiritual poverty',[3] a lack of connection where we think money spent on a just transition to a system which doesn't destroy is the loss, not the continued destruction itself. Solely pursuing money means a poverty of nature and of creativity, but it doesn't need to be this way.

Supporting rather than stripping back nature

If we look beyond that kind of thinking, it's exciting to play with what's possible. What if instead of an Amazon biome desecrated by cattle ranching partly funded by the leather industry,[4] the fashion industry could help support the rainforest, the Indigenous peoples and fellow animals who live there? Peruvian start-up Amazkin, created by Jorge Cajacuri and Ana Tafur, share a conservation agreement with seven Indigenous Awajún communities who protect nearly 3,000 hectares of the Amazonian rainforest. Together, this alliance uses Indigenous wisdom and artisanal practices to create a completely animal-free and petrochemical-free leather alternative, derived from the milky latex liquid which seeps out of Shiringa trees. Carved rings are formed around its trunk, allowing the latex to flow into a collection container without any harm to the tree and its growth. The collaboration exists to 'empower the consumer to see the Amazon through the lens of activism and conservation', the material an 'educational tool for intentional consumerism' that builds rather than breaks down.[5, 6]

There are many more examples of what we could do differently. What if all of our agricultural fruit waste really could be transformed into leather alternatives, providing additional income streams to farmers?[6]

What if Indonesian old-growth forests were not cut down for viscose production quite tight, because waste from the country's existing coconut industry was the feedstock for these materials instead?[7]

An Amazonian just transition

What if the existing efforts to improve leather tanneries, creating processes free from harmful substances, pollution and health hazards, was used to make mycelium leather as sustainable as it possibly could be? What if this meant keeping the tanning industry and its people alive and well, all the while preserving natural lands and cutting methane emissions tied to animal skin leather production?[6] What if farmlands full of sheep kept for wool growing were phased out through agricultural transitions and rewilding, used for carbon farming and ecotourism which better supported the wider community of people, as well as native animals, and the land they all stood on?[8]

What if those working in mines fuelling fast fashion's synthetic addiction instead worked in this kind of regeneration of land, life and community?[9] All of this innovation is happening now, albeit often at a small, community-level scale, waiting eagerly for further support.

A just transition is also not only about evolving materiality, but circularity. Imagine if we took less and made more with the many materials we already have – designing garments that can be disassembled and remade, making clothes from old clothes,[10] whether in our homes or in the factories of larger brands. What if we transitioned our thinking of 'repairs' as daggy and cheap, to customised, elevated and desirable?[10]

> What if old clothes were symbols of pride, adored more with each wear rather than tainted with boredom in a newness obsessed culture? What if we connected again with quality, craft, and how exceptionally brilliant the work of people who make clothes really is?

Perhaps the most exciting part of a recognition that we can justly transition away from harm is that we don't need to wait. We don't need to wait until we can produce as many responsible materials as we do for fossil fuel, animal-derived or other harmful materials today, because the scale of fashion production and purchasing is too large, no matter what we're making.[11] We can scale back, begin now, and make with the kind of care that garners citizen support which would keep businesses afloat.

We don't need to wait for other brands to get on board, for other people to dress the same way, because good fashion has never been about following trends: it's about creating, transforming, celebrating. We can make our own clothes, mend our clothes, reinvent our clothes, buy far fewer clothes which would allow us to afford clothes that did far less damage.

We all, whether participating in fashion through wearing, purchasing, making, designing, selling or promoting can help to change fashion. We can shift the industry away from constant fiscal growth and towards creative growth that remains profitable, while supporting environmental richness. And we can build systems and laws that demand this kind of change, so we aren't waiting for everyone with production power to realise the value of total ethics – because by then it will be too late. For those who think it's all a little far fetched, who think 'sweatshops provide employment' and that degrowth is poverty, perhaps we need to consider lives with a little more actual life and a little less work. Where our system produces less stuff for us, yet we have more time for ourselves, for ingenuity and creativity, for collaboration, and for nature.

A just transition towards total ethics may seem distant, even naive or out of reach. But if we don't stretch ourselves towards a goal of total ethics, of autonomy over domination, regeneration over destruction, nature over greed and creativity over exploitation, what are we doing? The work towards the 'impossible' that Dame Vivienne Westwood told us to demand in order to be reasonable is a place where we can find excitement, inspiration, passion and purpose.[12]

Total ethics fashion or bust.

11.
A call to action: the total ethics fashion manifesto

In the midst of interwoven environmental and ethical crises impacting the planet and all those of all species who share it, it is time for the fashion industry to transition towards a total ethics fashion system.

A total ethics fashion system prioritises the life and wellbeing of people, our fellow animals and the planet before profit and further production. In order for fashion to align with this premise, it must prioritise autonomy and consent: refusing the exploitation, commodification and destruction of all individuals and the planet we share. Ultimately, this means a just transition to a fashion system which pays living wages to everyone across all supply chains, which is slow, circular and respectful of planetary boundaries, and which shifts to sustainable and just alternatives to fossil fuel-based, native deforestation-driven and animal-derived materials alike.

A just transition towards a total ethics fashion system is complex and it takes time. It requires innovation, retraining, economic support, cultural sensitivity and a kind of progress which respects the value of tradition. It is required for sustained life on Earth. The total ethics fashion manifesto is not a demand that the fashion industry unfeasibly change overnight, but a recognition that a system which places all life before profit is the system we must continuously and boldly work towards through incremental yet radical and meaningful transformation.

Your signature

12.
What we can do next

If you wear clothes and buy clothes:

→ Try for less than five newly made garments, shoes and accessories each year. It's all that research suggests we and our Earth can actually afford or cope with.[1]

→ Look in your own wardrobe, in your friends' wardrobes, in vintage stores and on resale platforms before you look at buying new.

→ Treat your clothes, shoes and other fashionable things like you love them and want them to stay with you for a long time. Wash them cold, hang them out to dry, mend their holes, replace their soles, fold them carefully, remember everything it took for them to be in your life.

→ Look beyond fossil fuel- and animal-derived materials, and beyond materials tied to deforestation like uncertified viscose, too. Look for recycled, upcycled, plant-based, certified cellulosic, bio-based and other innovative materials when you're buying new.

→ Educate yourself. Talk to people about clothes, make it fashionable to consider your clothes, how they're made, by who and at what cost. Total ethics fashion needs to be desirable.

→ Remember that you have an impact beyond what you buy. Write to brands, tell them what you think, ask them to work towards total ethics. Be loud. Reclaim your power as a citizen, not only a consumer.

If you design, help to sell or exist in a business which makes and sells clothes:

You and everyone else will also fall into the first category of clothes-wearer,
unless you're a full-time nudist, which you probably are not.
But you can do more, too, given your relationship with fashion creation:

→   Get your brand to sign the total ethics manifesto
     at collectivefashionjustice.org/manifesto

→   Think beyond new seasons, new styles, newness, newness, newness.
     How can you design what already exists into something different?
     How can you design garments and a business which are designed for circularity
     and for the long term?

→   Phase out fossil fuel- and animal-derived materials as soon as possible,
     and push yourself with those targets. We can't afford not to move with urgency.
     Do the same for materials tied to deforestation, like uncertified viscose.

→   Prioritise paying every garment worker in your supply chain a living wage,
     and trace the entirety of your supply chain so you can work to ensure
     the same for everyone working across it. If we don't do this, we're profiting
     from poverty and sustained exploitation.

→   Talk about our fellow animals and our need to end our viewing of individuals
     as materials like it's a critical, unignorable part of creating a better,
     more sustainable and fair fashion industry – it is.

→   Think about the world view, the moral framework and the environment
     you are designing for your brand, not only the clothes you are designing.

→   Remember that designing less allows for designing better.

→   Practise truth-telling: be open about where you're at, where you want to be,
     and why it matters. Make this a communal practice where we work together.

If you hold a position of power where policy can be created and changed:

→ Get your council, city or state to sign the total ethics manifesto
    at collectivefashionjustice.org/manifesto, and sign it yourself, too.

→ Don't shy away from including ethical considerations in environmental policy:
    we need to if we're going to address environmental destruction holistically
    and effectively.

→ Push for more than transparency from the fashion industry.
    Push for more than long-term targets. Push for immediate action.

→ Be radical. We need you to be, to counteract the parts of the industry that aren't.

→ Ban the sale of wild animal-derived fashion, as a first step for other species.
    Ban deforestation-derived fashion. Ban fossil fuel-based fashion. Ban the sale
    of products made through labour injustices. Actions like these at small, local
    council levels add up. If you can't, ban the advertisement of these. If it seems
    impossible, think bigger, and create the steps to a place where it's possible.

→ Push for holistic, total ethics legislation, wherever you can.

→ Don't let infinite growth and rising consumption in fashion continue:
    we won't survive it.

→ Work with those at the grassroots.

→ End the subsidisation of harmful industries like fossil fuel mining
    and the animal industrial complex. Shift that funding towards
    a just transition to total ethics production.

Further information

If you want to learn more about total ethics fashion, different materials, the scale of fashion production and how it intersects with other issues, and how the wellbeing of people, our fellow animals and the planet relate to each other and to fashion, please head to the not-for-profit organisation I founded and direct, Collective Fashion Justice: collectivefashionjustice.org

If you want to help share the message of this book and the next steps we can take towards total ethics, consider sharing the information, resources and assets at: collectivefashionjustice.org/total-ethics-fashion-book

If you want digital, clickable references for this book (rather than the printed ones which follow), head to collectivefashionjustice.org/tef-book-refs

References

Introducing fashion, and our need for a total ethics fashion system

1. Pressman L. Fashion color trend report: New York Fashion Week autumn/winter 2021/2022. [Internet]. Carlstadt (US): Pantone; 2021 [cited 2023]. Available from: https://www.pantone.com/articles/fashion-color-trend-report/new-york-fashion-week-autumn-winter-2021-2022

2. Kelleher K. Bottega Veneta green was fashion's favourite colour. What happens next?. [Internet]. New York: Refinery 29; 2021 [cited 2023]. Available from: https://www.refinery29.com/en-au/2021/11/10766642/bottega-veneta-green

3. Bateman K. Breaking down the green trend sweeping the fashion world. [Internet]. New York; 2021 [cited 2023]. Available from: https://www.wmagazine.com/fashion/green-fashion-trend-explained

4. Adegeest D. How Bottega green became the trendiest colour in fashion. [Internet]. Amsterdam: Fashion United; 2021 [cited 2023]. Available from: https://fashionunited.uk/news/fashion/how-bottega-green-became-the-trendiest-colour-in-fashion/2021102158612

5. Afifa B. What is social media's impact on fast fashion? An investigation. [Internet]. Toronto: Fashion Takes Action; c2022 [cited 2023]. Available from: https://fashiontakesaction.com/articles/what-is-social-medias-impact-on-fast-fashion-an-investigation/

6. Unsustainable consumption of fashion. [Internet]. Melbourne: Collective Fashion Justice; 2022 [cited 2023]. Available from: https://www.collectivefashionjustice.org/mass-consumerism

7. de Freitas Netto S, Soral M, et al. 'Concepts and forms of green-washing: a systematic review.' *Environmental Sciences Europe.* 2020. 32: 19. https://enveurope.springeropen.com/articles/10.1186/s12302-020-0300-3

8. Delmas M, Burbano V. 'The drivers of greenwashing.' *California Management Review.* 2011. 54: 1; 64-87. https://journals.sagepub.com/doi/abs/10.1525/cmr.2011.54.1.64

9. Bryce E. Are clothes made from recycled materials really more sustainable?. [Internet]. London: The Guardian; 2021 [cited 2023]. Available from: https://www.theguardian.com/environment/2021/nov/06/clothes-made-from-recycled-materials-sustainable-plastic-climate

10. Synthetics anonymous: fashion brands' addiction to fossil fuels. [Internet]. London: Changing Markets Foundation; 2021 [cited 2023]. Available from: https://changingmarkets.org/wp-content/uploads/2021/07/SyntheticsAnonymous_FinalWeb.pdf

11. Rauturier S. What you need to know about fast fashion brands' 'eco' collections. [Internet]. Sydney: Good On You; 2021 [cited 2023]. Available from: https://goodonyou.eco/fast-fashion-eco-collections/

12. Truth about Fur. Sustainable fur – international fur federation. 2018 [cited 2023]. Available from: https://www.youtube.com/watch?v=-JC8HmyTRdg&t=4s

13. Hakansson E, Carter N, et al. Under their skin: leather's impact on the planet. [Internet]. Melbourne: Collective Fashion Justice; 2022 [cited 2023]. Available from: https://www.collectivefashionjustice.org/under-their-skin

14. L Booth, 'Environment and nature: the natural environment in Native American thought.' *Encyclopaedia of the History of Science, Technology, and Medicine in Non-Western Cultures.* 2008. 809-810. https://doi.org/10.1007/978-1-4020-4425-0_8568

15. Solomonian L, Di Ruggiero E. 'The critical intersection of environmental and social justice: a commentary.' *Globalization and Health.* 2021. 17: 30. https://globalizationandhealth.biomedcentral.com/articles/10.1186/s12992-021-00686-4

16. Cline E. Could living wages help solve fashion's climate crisis? New research says yes. [Internet]. Jersey City: Forbes; 2022 [cited 2023]. Available from: https://www.forbes.com/sites/elizabethlcline/2022/01/17/could-living-wages-help-solve-fashions-climate-crisis-new-research-says-yes/?sh=2097b6506b27

17. Warren K, Hadden J. The 15 richest people in the fashion industry, ranked. [Internet]. New York: Business Insider; 2020 [cited 2023]. Available from: https://www.businessinsider.com/the-richest-fashion-designers-and-brand-moguls-in-the-world-2017-9

18. Ritchie H. Humans make up just 0.01% of Earth's life – what's the rest?. [Internet]. Oxford: Our World in Data; 2019 [cited 2023]. Available from: https://ourworldindata.org/life-on-earth

19. Greenfield P, Benato M. Animal populations experience average decline of almost 70% since 1970, report reveals. [Internet]. London: The Guardian; 2022 [cited 2023]. Available from: https://www.theguardian.com/environment/2022/oct/13/almost-70-of-animal-populations-wiped-out-since-1970-report-reveals-aoe

20. Deforestation and biodiversity destruction for fashion. [Internet]. Melbourne: Collective Fashion Justice; 2022 [cited 2023]. Available from: https://www.collectivefashionjustice.org/deforestation-and-biodiversity

21. Hakansson E. Cruelty is out of fashion: an overview of the fashion industry's policies on wild animal products. [Internet]. Melbourne: Collective Fashion Justice; 2022 [cited 2023]. Available from: https://www.collectivefashionjustice.org/fashion-wild-animal-exploitation

22. The science of animal welfare. [Internet]. San Francisco: Faunalytics; 2016 [cited 2023]. Available from: https://faunalytics.org/science-animal-welfare/

23. Hakansson E, Halliday C, et al. Under their skin: leather's impact on animals. [Internet]. Melbourne: Collective Fashion Justice; 2023 [cited 2023]. Available from: https://www.collectivefashionjustice.org/under-their-skin

24. Non-human animals. [Internet]. Melbourne: Collective Fashion Justice; c2023 [cited 2023]. Available from: https://www.collectivefashionjustice.org/non-humans

25. Greenhouse gas emissions. [Internet]. Melbourne: Collective Fashion Justice; c2023 [cited 2023]. Available from: https://www.collectivefashionjustice.org/greenhouse-gas-emissions

26. Human animals. [Internet]. Melbourne: Collective Fashion Justice; c2023 [cited 2023]. Available from: https://www.collectivefashionjustice.org/humans

27. Hakansson E, Vance U, et al. Under their skin: leather's impact on people. [Internet]. Melbourne: Collective Fashion Justice; 2022 [cited 2023]. Available from: https://www.collectivefashionjustice.org/under-their-skin

Where fashion is today

1. Morriss-Kay G. 'The evolution of human artistic creativity.' *Journal of Anatomy*. 2009. 216 (2): 158-176. https://doi.org/10.1111%2Fj.1469-7580.2009.01160.x

2. Remy N, Speelman E, Swartz S. Style that's sustainable: a new fast-fashion formula. [Internet]. Paris: McKinsey; 2016 [cited 2023]. Available from: https://www.mckinsey.com/capabilities/sustainability/our-insights/style-thats-sustainable-a-new-fast-fashion-formula

References

3. Day of 8 billion. [Internet]. Geneva: United Nations; 2022 [cited 2023].
    Available from: https://www.un.org/en/dayof8billion

4. Monroe R. Ultra-fast fashion is eating the world. [Internet].
    Washington: The Atlantic; 2021 [cited 2023].
    Available from: https://www.theatlantic.com/magazine/archive/2021/03/ultra-fast-fashion-is-eating-the-world/617794/

5. Kelly C. Australians buy almost 15kg of clothes every year and most of it ends up in landfill,
    report finds. [Internet]. Sydney: Guardian Australia; 2022 [cited 2023].
    Available from: https://www.theguardian.com/australia-news/2022/jul/20/australians-buy-almost-15kg-of-clothes-every-year-and-most-of-it-ends-up-in-landfill-report-finds

6. Algamal A. New shocking facts about the impact of fast fashion on our climate. [Internet].
    Oxford: Oxfam; 2019 [cited 2023]. Available from: https://www.oxfam.org.uk/oxfam-in-action/oxfam-blog/new-shocking-facts-about-the-impact-of-fast-fashion-on-our-climate/

7. Loetscher S. Changing fashion: the clothing and textile industry at the brink of radical
    transformation. [Internet]. Zurich: WWF Switzerland; 2017 [cited 2023].
    Available from: https://www.wwf.ch/sites/default/files/doc-2017-09/2017-09-WWF-Report-Changing_fashion_2017_EN.pdf

8. Textiles in Europe's circular economy. [Internet].
    Copenhagen: European Environmental Agency; 2023 [cited 2023].
    Available from: https://www.eea.europa.eu/publications/textiles-in-europes-circular-economy

9. A new textile economy: redesigning fashion's future. [Internet].
    Isle of Wight (GB): Ellen Macarthur Foundation; 2017 [cited 2023].
    Available from: https://ellenmacarthurfoundation.org/a-new-textiles-economy

10. Teh C. A mountain of unsold clothing from fast-fashion retailers is piling up in the Chilean desert.
    [Internet]. New York: Business Insider; 2021 [cited 2023].
    Available from: https://www.insider.com/discarded-fast-fashion-clothes-chile-desert-2021-11

11. Unsustainable consumption of fashion. [Internet]. Melbourne: Collective Fashion Justice; 2022
    [cited 2023]. Available from: https://www.collectivefashionjustice.org/mass-consumerism

12. Kokoroko F, Inveen C. Ghana's vintage enthusiasts give new life to Western clothing waste. [Internet].
    London: Reuters; 2023 [cited 2023]. Available from: https://www.reuters.com/lifestyle/ghanas-vintage-enthusiasts-give-new-life-western-clothing-waste-2022-12-28/

13. Besser L. Dead white man's clothes. [Internet]. Sydney: ABC News; 2021 [cited 2023].
    Available from: https://www.abc.net.au/news/2021-08-12/fast-fashion-turning-parts-ghana-into-toxic-landfill/100358702

14. Ricketts L. This is not your goldmine. This is our mess. [Internet]. New York: Atmos; 2021 [cited 2023].
    Available from: https://atmos.earth/fashion-clothing-waste-letter-ghana/

15. Simpliciano L, Galvin M, et al. Fashion Transparency Index 2022. [Internet]. London: Fashion
    Revolution; 2022 [cited 2023]. Available from: https://issuu.com/fashionrevolution/docs/fti_2022

16. Preferred fiber and materials market report 2021. [Internet]. Lamesa (US): Textile Exchange; 2021
    [cited 2023]. Available from: https://textileexchange.org/app/uploads/2021/08/Textile-Exchange_Preferred-Fiber-and-Materials-Market-Report_2021.pdf

17. Hakansson E. The IPCC's mitigation of climate change report explained, and what it means for
    the fashion industry. [Internet]. Melbourne: Collective Fashion Justice; 2022 [cited 2023].
    Available from: https://www.collectivefashionjustice.org/articles/the-ipccs-mitigation-of-climate-change-report-explained-and-what-it-means-for-the-fashion-industry

18. Fossil fashion: the hidden reliance of fast fashion on fossil fuels. [Internet]. London: Changing Markets Foundation; 2021 [cited 2023]. Available from: https://changingmarkets.org/wp-content/uploads/2021/01/FOSSIL-FASHION_Web-compressed.pdf

19. Boele R, Brodie M, et al. Resources, energy and modern slavery. [Internet]. Sydney: Australian Human Rights Commission; 2021 [cited 2023]. Available from: https://humanrights.gov.au/sites/default/files/document/publication/ahrc_kpmg_modern_slavery_energy_2021_.pdf

20. Global slavery index. [Internet]. Perth: Walk Free; 2018 [cited 2023]. Available from: https://www.globalslaveryindex.org/2018/data/maps/#prevalence

21. Palacios-Mateo C, van der Meer Y, et al. 'Analysis of the polyester clothing value chain to identify key intervention points for sustainability.' *Environmental Sciences Europe.* 2021. 33: 2. https://enveurope.springeropen.com/articles/10.1186/s12302-020-00447-x

22. Stanes F, Gibson C. Materials that linger: an embodied geography of polyester clothes. [Internet]. Wollongong (AU): University of Wollongong; 2017 [cited 2023]. Available from: https://ro.uow.edu.au/cgi/viewcontent.cgi?article=4097&context=sspapers&httpsredir=1&referer=

23. Ingraffia R, Amato G, et al. 'Polyester microplastic fibers in soil increase nitrogen loss via leaching and decrease plant biomass production and N uptake.' *Environmental Research Letters.* 2022. 17: 5. https://doi.org/10.1088/1748-9326/ac652d

24. Sabanoglu T. Share in world exports of the leading clothing exporters 2021, by country. [Internet]. Hamburg: Statista; 2022 [cited 2023]. Available from: https://www.statista.com/statistics/1094515/share-of-the-leading-global-textile-clothing-by-country/

25. Garment workers. [Internet]. Melbourne: Collective Fashion Justice; 2022 [cited 2023]. Available from: https://www.collectivefashionjustice.org/garment-workers

26. San Segundo I. Do you know how much garment workers really make?. [Internet]. London: Fashion Revolution; 2020 [cited 2023]. Available from: https://www.fashionrevolution.org/usa-blog/how-much-garment-workers-really-make/

27. Greenley R. This is the reality of America's fast-fashion addiction. [Internet]. New York: The New York Times; 2022 [cited 2023]. Available from: https://www.nytimes.com/2022/11/25/opinion/warehouse-fastfashion-return.html

28. Pullar J. Just 10% of fashion brands pay their factory workers a living wage. [Internet]. Sydney: Elle Australia; 2022 [cited 2023]. Available from: https://www.elle.com.au/fashion/ethical-fashion-wages-27836

29. Jackson S. Shein factory employees are working 18-hour days for pennies per garment and washing their hair on lunch breaks because they have so little time off, new report finds. [Internet]. New York: Business Insider; 2022 [cited 2023]. Available from: https://www.businessinsider.com/shein-factory-workers-18-hour-shifts-paid-low-wages-report-2022-10

30. Hakansson E, Carter N, et al. Under their skin: leather's impact on the planet. [Internet]. Melbourne: Collective Fashion Justice; 2022 [cited 2023]. Available from: https://www.collectivefashionjustice.org/under-their-skin

31. Hakansson E, Vance U, et al. Under their skin: leather's impact on people. [Internet]. Melbourne: Collective Fashion Justice; 2022 [cited 2023]. Available from: https://www.collectivefashionjustice.org/under-their-skin

32. Hakansson E, Halliday C, et al. Under their skin: leather's impact on animals. [Internet]. Melbourne: Collective Fashion Justice; 2023 [cited 2023]. Available from: https://www.collectivefashionjustice.org/under-their-skin

33. Slaughterhouse workers. [Internet]. Melbourne: Collective Fashion Justice; 2022 [cited 2023]. Available from: https://www.collectivefashionjustice.org/slaughterhouse-workers

34. Lebwohl M. A call to action: psychological harm in slaughterhouse workers. [Internet]. [Connecticut]: Yale Global Health Review; 2016 [cited 2023]. Available from: https://yaleglobalhealthreview.com/2016/01/25/a-call-to-action-psychological-harm-in-slaughterhouse-workers/

35. Fitzgerald A, Kalof L, et al. 'Slaughterhouses and increased crime rates: an empirical analysis of the spillover from 'the jungle' into the surrounding community.' *Organization and Environment*. 2009. https://doi.org/10.1177/1086026609338164

36. SSIP is attempting to measure the biodegradability. [Internet]. Milan: Tannery Magazine; 2017 [cited 2023]. Available from: https://tannerymagazine.com/ssip-biodegradability/

37. Hashmi G, Dastageer G, et al. 'Leather industry and environment: Pakistan scenario.' 2017. 1 (2): 20-25. Available from: https://www.researchgate.net/publication/317381731_Leather_Industry_and_Environment_Pakistan_Scenario

How we view fashion and sustainability

1. Lu Sheng. Clean energy and the fashion supply chain – latest corporate strategies. [Internet]. Bromsgrove: Just Style; 2021 [cited 2023]. Available from: https://www.just-style.com/features/free-to-read-clean-energy-and-the-fashion-supply-chain-latest-corporate-strategies/

2. Deeley R. Fashion's race for new materials. [Internet]. London: Business of Fashion; 2022 [cited 2023]. Available from: https://www.businessoffashion.com/case-studies/sustainability/materials-innovation-textiles-recycling-production/

3. Granskog A, Laizet F, et al. Biodiversity: the next frontier in sustainable fashion. [Internet]. Helsinki: McKinsey; 2020 [cited 2023]. Available from: https://www.mckinsey.com/industries/retail/our-insights/biodiversity-the-next-frontier-in-sustainable-fashion

4. Brand engagement with next-gen materials: 2022 landscape. [Internet]. San Francisco: Material Innovation Initiative; 2022 [cited 2023]. Available from: https://materialinnovation.org/wp-content/uploads/Next-Gen-Materials_Brand-Engagement-Report_FINAL_2-1-2022.pdf

5. Hakansson E. The IPCC's mitigation of climate change report explained, and what it means for the fashion industry. [Internet]. Melbourne: Collective Fashion Justice; 2022 [cited 2023]. Available from: https://www.collectivefashionjustice.org/articles/the-ipccs-mitigation-of-climate-change-report-explained-and-what-it-means-for-the-fashion-industry

6. Synthetics. [Internet]. Melbourne: Collective Fashion Justice; 2022 [cited 2023]. Available from: https://www.collectivefashionjustice.org/synthetics

7. Poore J, Nemecek T. 'Reducing food's environmental impacts through producers and consumers.' *Science*. 2018. 360: 6392. 987-992. https://doi.org/10.1126/science.aaq0216

8. Planet. [Internet]. Melbourne: Collective Fashion Justice; 2022 [cited 2023]. Available from: https://www.collectivefashionjustice.org/planet

9. Jacquet J. The meat industry is doing exactly what Big Oil does to fight climate action. [Internet]. Washington: The Washington Post; 2021 [cited 2023]. Available from: https://www.washingtonpost.com/outlook/the-meat-industry-is-doing-exactly-what-big-oil-does-to-fight-climate-action/2021/05/14/831e14be-b3fe-11eb-ab43-bebddc5a0f65_story.html

10. Causes and effects of climate change. [Internet]. Geneva: United Nations; c2023 [cited 2023].
    Available from: https://www.un.org/en/climatechange/science/causes-effects-climate-change

11. Shukla P, Skea J, et al. Climate change 2022: mitigation of climate change. [Internet]. Nairobi: United
    Nations Environmental Programme; 2022 [cited 2023].
    Available from: https://www.ipcc.ch/report/ar6/wg3/downloads/report/IPCC_AR6_WGIII_FullReport.pdf

12. Jackson R, Saunois M, et al. 'Increasing anthropogenic methane emissions arise equally
    from agricultural and fossil fuel sources.' Environmental Research Letters. 2020. 15.
    https://doi.org/10.1088/1748-9326/ab9ed2

13. Lu X. Jacob D, et al. 'Global methane budget and trend, 2010–2017: complementarity of inverse
    analyses using in situ (GLOBALVIEWplus CH4 ObsPack) and satellite (GOSAT) observations.'
    Atmospheric Chemistry and Physics. 2021. 21: 6. 4637-4657. https://doi.org/10.5194/acp-21-4637-2021

14. Howarth R. 'Methane emissions from fossil fuels: exploring recent changes in greenhouse-gas
    reporting requirements for the State of New York.' Journal of Integrative Environmental Sciences.
    2019. 17: 3. 69-81. https://doi.org/10.1080/1943815X.2020.1789666

15. Rearing cattle produces more greenhouse gases than driving cars, UN report warns. [Internet].
    Rome: United Nations Food and Agriculture Organization; 2006 [cited 2023].
    Available from: https://news.un.org/en/story/2006/11/201222-rearing-cattle-produces-more-
    greenhouse-gases-driving-cars-un-report-warns

16. Hakansson E, Carter N, et al. Under their skin: leather's impact on the planet. [Internet].
    Melbourne: Collective Fashion Justice; 2022 [cited 2023].
    Available from: https://www.collectivefashionjustice.org/under-their-skin

17. Wool. [Internet]. Melbourne: Collective Fashion Justice; 2022 [cited 2023].
    Available from: https://www.collectivefashionjustice.org/wool

18. Shear destruction. [Internet]. Melbourne: Collective Fashion Justice; 2021 [cited 2023].
    Available from: https://www.collectivefashionjustice.org/shear-destruction

19. Hakansson E. How do wool, lyocell and cotton knitwear compare, when it comes to land impact?.
    [Internet]. Melbourne: Circumfauna; 2022 [cited 2023].
    Available from: https://circumfauna.org/fibre-land-comparisons

20. Uncertified cellulose. [Internet]. Melbourne: Collective Fashion Justice; 2022 [cited 2023].
    Available from: https://www.collectivefashionjustice.org/uncertified-cellulose

21. Roberts-Islam B. 'Silenced data' means we don't know global impacts of cotton pesticides.
    [Internet]. Jersey City: Forbes; 2021 [cited 2023].
    Available from: https://www.forbes.com/sites/brookerobertsislam/2021/12/06/silenced-data-means-
    we-dont-know-global-impacts-of-cotton-pesticides/?sh=244c3bf4668b

22. Holgate B. Microfibre pollution in fashion: are synthetics all to blame?. [Internet].
    Melbourne: Collective Fashion Justice; 2021 [cited 2023].
    Available from: https://www.collectivefashionjustice.org/articles/microfibre-pollution-in-fashion-
    are-synthetics-all-to-blame

23. Al-Tohamy R, Ali S, et al. 'A critical review on the treatment of dye-containing wastewater:
    ecotoxicological and health concerns of textile dyes and possible remediation approaches
    for environmental safety.' Ecotoxicology and Environmental Safety. 2022. 231.
    https://doi.org/10.1016/j.ecoenv.2021.113160

24. Survey: consumers want sustainable clothing. [Internet]. San Diego: Geno; 2021 [cited 2023].
    Available from: https://www.genomatica.com/news-content/survey-consumers-want-sustainable-
    clothing/

References

25. Consumers are confused about what 'sustainability' means in fashion, per new survey. [Internet]. New York: The Fashion Law; 2021 [cited 2023]. Available from: https://www.thefashionlaw.com/consumers-are-confused-about-what-sustainability-means-in-fashion-per-new-survey/

26. Mandarić D, Hunjet A, et al. 'Perception of consumers' awareness about sustainability of fashion brands.' *Journal of Risk and Financial Management*. 2021. 14 (12): 594. https://doi.org/10.3390/jrfm14120594

27. Sustainable fashion: a survey on global perspectives. [Internet]. Central Hong Kong: KPMG; 2019 [cited 2023]. Available from: https://assets.kpmg.com/content/dam/kpmg/cn/pdf/en/2019/01/sustainable-fashion.pdf

28. Unsustainable consumption of fashion. [Internet]. Melbourne: Collective Fashion Justice; 2022 [cited 2023]. Available from: https://www.collectivefashionjustice.org/mass-consumerism

29. Webb B. Degrowth: the future that fashion has been looking for?/ [Internet]. London: Vogue Business; 2022 [cited 2023]. Available from: https://www.voguebusiness.com/sustainability/degrowth-the-future-that-fashion-has-been-looking-for

30. What is a circular economy?. [Internet]. Isle of Wight (GB): Ellen Macarthur Foundation; c2023 [cited 2023]. Available from: https://ellenmacarthurfoundation.org/topics/circular-economy-introduction/overview

31. Konietzko J. Moving beyond carbon tunnel vision with a sustainability data strategy. [Internet]. Jersey City; 2022 [cited 2023]. Available from: https://www.forbes.com/sites/cognizant/2022/04/07/moving-beyond-carbon-tunnel-vision-with-a-sustainability-data-strategy/?sh=57ded0cc70a7

32. Greenhouse gas emissions. [Internet]. Melbourne: Collective Fashion Justice; 2022 [cited 2023]. Available from: https://www.collectivefashionjustice.org/greenhouse-gas-emissions

33. Thomas L. As a black environmentalist, I wanted so much more from COP26. [Internet]. New York: Vogue; 2021 [cited 2023]. Available from: https://www.vogue.com/article/as-a-black-environmentalist-i-wanted-so-much-more-from-cop26

How we view fashion and ethics

1. Chanel T. How fast-fashion and racism are intricately linked. [Internet]. San Francisco: Remake.world; 2020 [cited 2023]. Available from: https://remake.world/stories/news/how-fast-fashion-and-racism-are-intricately-linked/

2. Hakansson E, Vance U, et al. Under their skin: leather's impact on people. [Internet]. Melbourne: Collective Fashion Justice; 2022 [cited 2023]. Available from: https://www.collectivefashionjustice.org/under-their-skin

3. Indigenous land rights. [Internet]. Melbourne: Collective Fashion Justice; 2022 [cited 2023]. Available from: https://www.collectivefashionjustice.org/indigenous-land-rights

4. Rana Plaza. [Internet]. Amsterdam: Clean Clothes Campaign; c2023 [cited 2023]. Available from: https://cleanclothes.org/campaigns/past/rana-plaza

5. Garment workers. [Internet]. Melbourne: Collective Fashion Justice; 2022 [cited 2023]. Available from: https://www.collectivefashionjustice.org/garment-workers

6. Legesse K. Racism is at the heart of fast fashion – it's time for change. [Internet]. London: The Guardian; 2020 [cited 2023]. Available from: https://www.theguardian.com/global-development/2020/jun/11/racism-is-at-the-heart-of-fast-fashion-its-time-for-change

7. Silk. [Internet]. Melbourne: Collective Fashion Justice; 2022 [cited 2023]. Available from: https://www.collectivefashionjustice.org/silk

8. Kannuri N, Jadhav S. 'Generating toxic landscapes: impact on well-being of cotton farmers in Telangana, India.' *Anthropology and Medicine*. 2018. 25: 1. 121-140. https://doi.org/10.1080/13648470.2017.1317398

9. Wool. [Internet]. Melbourne: Collective Fashion Justice; 2022 [cited 2023]. Available from: https://www.collectivefashionjustice.org/wool

10. Cashmere. [Internet]. Melbourne: Collective Fashion Justice; 2022 [cited 2023]. Available from: https://www.collectivefashionjustice.org/cashmere

11. Bales K, Sovacool B. 'From forests to factories: how modern slavery deepens the crisis of climate change.' *Energy Research and Social Science*. 2021. 77. https://doi.org/10.1016/j.erss.2021.102096

12. Deforestation and biodiversity. [Internet]. Melbourne: Collective Fashion Justice; 2022 [cited 2023]. Available from: https://www.collectivefashionjustice.org/deforestation-and-biodiversity

13. Leather. [Internet]. Melbourne: Collective Fashion Justice; 2022 [cited 2023]. Available from: https://www.collectivefashionjustice.org/leather

14. Uncertified cellulose. Melbourne: Collective Fashion Justice; 2022 [cited 2023]. Available from: https://www.collectivefashionjustice.org/uncertified-cellulose

15. Hakansson E, Carter N, et al. Under their skin: leather's impact on the planet. [Internet]. Melbourne: Collective Fashion Justice; 2022 [cited 2023]. Available from: https://www.collectivefashionjustice.org/under-their-skin

16. Greenfield P, Benato M. Animal populations experience average decline of almost 70% since 1970, report reveals. [Internet]. London: The Guardian; 2022 [cited 2023]. Available from: https://www.theguardian.com/environment/2022/oct/13/almost-70-of-animal-populations-wiped-out-since-1970-report-reveals-aoe

17. World statistical compendium for raw hides and skins, leather and leather footwear 1999-2015. [Internet]. Rome: United Nations Food and Agricultural Organization; 2016 [cited 2023]. Available from: https://www.fao.org/3/i5599e/i5599e.pdf

18. Crops and livestock products. [Internet]. Rome: United Nations Food and Agricultural Organization; 2020 [cited 2022]. Available from: https://www.fao.org/faostat/en/#data/QCL

19. Hakansson E. Cruelty is out of fashion: an overview of the fashion industry's policies on wild animal products. [Internet]. Melbourne: Collective Fashion Justice; 2022 [cited 2023]. Available from: https://www.collectivefashionjustice.org/fashion-wild-animal-exploitation

20. Non-human animals. [Internet]. Melbourne: Collective Fashion Justice; 2022 [cited 2023]. Available from: https://www.collectivefashionjustice.org/non-humans

21. Low P, Panksepp J, Reiss D, et al. The Cambridge Declaration on Consciousness. [Internet]. Cambridge: Francis Crick Memorial Conference; 2012 [cited 2023]. Available from: http://fcmconference.org/img/CambridgeDeclarationOnConsciousness.pdf

22. Donatella Versace signals end to use of real fur at fashion label. [Internet]. London: The Guardian; 2018 [cited 2023]. Available from: https://www.theguardian.com/fashion/2018/mar/15/donatella-versace-signals-real-fur-fashion-label

References

23. Hakansson E, Halliday C, et al. Under their skin: leather's impact on animals. [Internet]. Melbourne: Collective Fashion Justice; 2023 [cited 2023]. Available from: https://www.collectivefashionjustice.org/under-their-skin

24. Hakansson E. How veganism can save us. Melbourne: Hardie Grant; 2022.

25. Joy M. Why we love dogs, eat pigs, and wear cows: an introduction to carnism. Miami: Conari Press; 2009.

26. Hakansson E. Is the Responsible Wool Standard cruelty free? Is the ZQ wool certification free from harm?. [Internet]. Melbourne: Collective Fashion Justice; 2021 [cited 2023]. Available from: https://www.collectivefashionjustice.org/articles/wool-standards-explained

27. Down. [Internet]. Melbourne: Collective Fashion Justice; 2022 [cited 2023]. Available from: https://www.collectivefashionjustice.org/down

28. The Responsible Down Standard aims to protect ducks and geese used for down. [Internet]. Lamesa (US): Textile Exchange; c2022 [cited 2023]. Available from: https://textileexchange.org/responsible-down-standard/

29. Hakansson E. What is the Leather Working Group certification, and does it make for sustainable and ethical leather?. [Internet]. Melbourne: Collective Fashion Justice; 2022 [cited 2023]. Available from: https://www.collectivefashionjustice.org/articles/what-is-the-leather-working-group-certification-and-does-it-make-for-sustainable-and-ethical-leather

30. Hakansson E. How to spot ethics-washing. [Internet]. Melbourne: Collective Fashion Justice; 2022 [cited 2023]. Available from: https://www.collectivefashionjustice.org/articles/how-to-spot-ethics-washing

31. Safe sheep handling guide. [Internet]. Wellington: WorkSafe New Zealand; 2017 [cited 2023]. Available from: https://www.worksafe.govt.nz/topic-and-industry/agriculture/working-with-animals/working-with-sheep/safe-sheep-handling-gpg/

32. Code of practice for the care and handling of farmed fox. [Internet]. Lacombe (CA): National Farm Animal Care Council; 2013 [cited 2023]. Available from: https://www.nfacc.ca/codes-of-practice/farmed-fox-code

33. Code of practice on the humane treatment of wild and farmed Australian crocodiles. [Internet]. Canberra: Natural Resource Management Ministerial Council; 2009 [cited 2023]. Available from: https://www.dcceew.gov.au/sites/default/files/documents/crocodile-code-practice.pdf

34. Moran C. Trying to breed the 'aggression' out of cattle. [Internet]. Dublin: Agriland; 2016 [cited 2023]. Available from: https://www.agriland.ie/farming-news/trying-to-breed-the-aggression-out-of-cattle/

35. Haskell M, Simm G, et al. 'Genetic selection for temperament traits in dairy and beef cattle.' Frontiers in Genetics. 2014. 5. https://www.frontiersin.org/articles/10.3389/fgene.2014.00368/full

36. Genetic estimates for temperament traits in sheep breeds. [Internet]. Sydney: Meat and Livestock Australia; 2007 [cited 2023]. Available from: https://www.mla.com.au/research-and-development/reports/2005/genetic-estimates-for-temperament-traits-in-sheep-breeds/

Sustaining injustice

1.   Hudd A. Dyeing for fashion: why the clothes industry is causing 20% of water pollution. [Internet].
     Lyon (FR): Euronews; 2022 [cited 2023]. Available from: https://www.euronews.com/
     green/2022/02/26/dyeing-for-fashion-why-the-fashion-industry-is-causing-20-of-water-pollution

2.   Hakansson E, Halliday C, et al. Under their skin: leather's impact on animals. [Internet].
     Melbourne: Collective Fashion Justice; 2023 [cited 2023].
     Available from: https://www.collectivefashionjustice.org/under-their-skin

3.   Wool. [Internet]. Melbourne: Collective Fashion Justice; 2022 [cited 2023].
     Available from: https://www.collectivefashionjustice.org/wool

4.   Sparrow J. Eco-fascists and the ugly fight for 'our way of life' as the environment disintegrates.
     [Internet]. London: The Guardian; 2019 [cited 2023].
     Available from: https://www.theguardian.com/environment/2019/nov/30/eco-fascists-and-the-ugly-
     fight-for-our-way-of-life-as-the-environment-disintegrates

5.   Dominguez R, Naimark J, et al. Eco-fascism: a tangible and present danger. [Internet].
     Washington: Earthworks; 2022 [cited 2023].
     Available from: https://earthworks.org/blog/eco-fascism-a-tangible-present-danger/

6.   Crocodile skin. [Internet]. Melbourne: Collective Fashion Justice; 2022 [cited 2023].
     Available from: https://www.collectivefashionjustice.org/crocodile-skin

7.   Drop croc. [Internet]. Melbourne: Collective Fashion Justice; 2021 [cited 2023].
     Available from: https://www.collectivefashionjustice.org/drop-croc

8.   Donaghy T, Jiang C, et al. Fossil fuel racism. [Internet]. Washington: Greenpeace; 2022 [cited 2023].
     Available from: https://www.greenpeace.org/usa/wp-content/uploads/2021/04/Fossil-Fuel-Racism.pdf

9.   Synthetics. [Internet]. Melbourne: Collective Fashion Justice; 2022 [cited 2023].
     Available from: https://www.collectivefashionjustice.org/synthetics

10. Hakansson E, Vance U, et al. Under their skin: leather's impact on people. [Internet].

11. Melbourne: Collective Fashion Justice; 2022 [cited 2023].
     Available from: https://www.collectivefashionjustice.org/under-their-skin

12. Bales K, Sovacool B. 'From forests to factories: how modern slavery deepens the crisis of climate
     change.' *Energy Research and Social Science*. 2021. 77. https://doi.org/10.1016/j.erss.2021.102096

13. Cline E. Could living wages help solve fashion's climate crisis? New research says yes. [Internet].
     Jersey City: Forbes; 2022 [cited 2023]. Available from: https://www.forbes.com/sites/
     elizabethlcline/2022/01/17/could-living-wages-help-solve-fashions-climate-crisis-new-research-
     says-yes/?sh=2097b6506b27

14. Conventional cotton. [Internet]. Melbourne: Collective Fashion Justice; 2022 [cited 2023].
     Available from: https://www.collectivefashionjustice.org/conventional-cotton

15. Fragar L, Temperley J. The impact of biotechnology and other factors on health and safety
     in the Australian cotton industry. [Internet]. Sydney: The University of Sydney; 2008 [cited 2023].
     Available from: https://aghealth.sydney.edu.au/wp-content/uploads/2019/05/impact_of_
     biotechnology_in_cotton_final_110208.pdf

16. Kouser S, Qaim M. 'Impact of Bt cotton on pesticide poisoning in smallholder agriculture: a panel data
     analysis.' *Ecological Economics*. 2011. 70: 11. 2105-2113. https://doi.org/10.1016/j.ecolecon.2011.06.008

17. Ritchie H. If the world adopted a plant-based diet we would reduce global agricultural land use from 4 to 1 billion hectares. [Internet]. Oxford: Our World in Data; 2021 [cited 2023]. Available from: https://ourworldindata.org/land-use-diets

18. Hayek M, Harwatt H, et al. 'The carbon opportunity cost of animal-soured food production on land.' *Nature Sustainability.* 2020. 4. 21-24. https://doi.org/10.1038/s41893-020-00603-4

19. Meredith S. The world's in a 'polycrisis' – and these countries want to quash it by looking beyond GDP. [Internet]. Englewood Cliffs (US): CNBC; 2022 [cited 2023]. Available from: https://www.cnbc.com/2022/12/26/well-being-these-countries-are-looking-beyond-gdp-and-economic-growth.html

20. Tobin K, Aguilar A. Beyond GDP: alternatives to capitalism already exist. [Internet]. Washington: Greenpeace; 2022 [cited 2023]. Available from: https://www.greenpeace.org/international/story/54859/beyond-gdpalternatives-to-capitalism-already-exist/

21. Lee B, Butler B. Sorry, GDP. There are other ways to measure a nation's worth. [Internet]. London: WIRED; 2023 [cited 2023]. Available from: https://www.wired.co.uk/article/happiness-measurement-humanity

22. Hickel J. The World Bank is upset that Bhutan's old-growth forests are just standing there, doing nothing, when they could be turned into Ikea furniture. [Internet]. San Francisco: Twitter; 2020 [cited 2023]. Available from: https://twitter.com/jasonhickel/status/1317028075947892736?lang=en

23. Nugent C. Amsteerdam is embracing a radical new economic theory to help save the environment. Could it also replace capitalism?. [Internet]. New York: Time; 2021 [cited 2023]. Available from: https://time.com/5930093/amsterdam-doughnut-economics/

24. About doughnut economics. [Internet]. Oxford: Doughnut Economics Action Lab; c2023 [cited 2023]. Available from: https://doughnuteconomics.org/about-doughnut-economics

25. Munro C. Is it possible to be anti-capitalist and love fashion? It's complicated. [Internet]. New York: Refinery 29; 2020 [cited 2023]. Available from: https://www.refinery29.com/en-us/fashion-social-change-brands-anti-capitalism

Total ethics fashion explained

1. Chiu A. 'Vegan', 'sustainable', how to spot misleading fashion claims. [Internet]. Washington: The Washington Post; 2023 [cited 2023]. Available from: https://www.washingtonpost.com/climate-solutions/2023/01/25/greenwashing-fashion-clothes-vegan-sustainable/

2. Shear destruction. [Internet]. Melbourne: Collective Fashion Justice; 2021 [cited 2023]. Available from: https://www.collectivefashionjustice.org/shear-destruction

3. Wool. [Internet]. Melbourne: Collective Fashion Justice; 2022 [cited 2023]. Available from: https://www.collectivefashionjustice.org/wool

4. Indigenous land rights. [Internet]. Melbourne: Collective Fashion Justice; 2022 [cited 2023]. Available from: https://www.collectivefashionjustice.org/indigenous-land-rights

5. Hakansson E, Halliday C, et al. Under their skin: leather's impact on animals. [Internet]. Melbourne: Collective Fashion Justice; 2023 [cited 2023]. Available from: https://www.collectivefashionjustice.org/under-their-skin

6.   Conventional cotton. [Internet]. Melbourne: Collective Fashion Justice; 2022 [cited 2023].
     Available from: https://www.collectivefashionjustice.org/conventional-cotton

7.   Hakansson E, Carter N, et al. Under their skin: leather's impact on the planet. [Internet].
     Melbourne: Collective Fashion Justice; 2023 [cited 2023].
     Available from: https://www.collectivefashionjustice.org/under-their-skin

Humans as animals

8.   Ritchie H. Humans make up just 0.01% of Earth's life – what's the rest?. [Internet].
     Oxford: Our World in Data; 2019 [cited 2023]. Available from: https://ourworldindata.org/life-on-earth

9.   Hakansson E, Halliday C, et al. Under their skin: leather's impact on animals. [Internet].

10. Melbourne: Collective Fashion Justice; 2023 [cited 2023].
     Available from: https://www.collectivefashionjustice.org/under-their-skin

11. Marino L, Merskin D. 'Intelligence, complexity and individuality in sheep.'
     Animal Sentience. 2019. 25: 1. Available from: https://www.wellbeingintlstudiesrepository.org/cgi/
     viewcontent.cgi?article=1374&context=animsent

12. Bekoff M. The rich emotional lives of chimpanzees and goats. [Internet].
     New York: Psychology Today; 2019 [cited 2023]. Available from: https://www.psychologytoday.com/
     us/blog/animal-emotions/201907/the-rich-emotional-lives-chimpanzees-and-goats

13. Singer P. *Practical ethics.* Cambridge: Cambridge University Press; 1979.

14. Monsó S, Benz-Schwarzburg J, et al. 'Animal morality: what it means and why it matters.' *The Journal
     of Ethics.* 2018. 22: 3. 283-310. https://doi.org/10.1007%2Fs10892-018-9275-3

15. Simpliciano L, Galvin M, et al. Fashion Transparency Index 2022. [Internet]. London: Fashion
     Revolution; 2022 [cited 2023]. Available from: https://issuu.com/fashionrevolution/docs/fti_2022

16. Freire P. *Pedagogy of the oppressed.* New York: The Continuum International Publishing Group. 2005.

17. Hakansson E. *How veganism can save us.* Melbourne: Hardie Grant; 2022.

18. Slaughterhouse workers. [Internet]. Melbourne: Collective Fashion Justice; 2022 [cited 2023].
     Available from: https://www.collectivefashionjustice.org/slaughterhouse-workers

19. Hakansson E, Vance U, et al. Under their skin: leather's impact on people. [Internet].
     Melbourne: Collective Fashion Justice; 2022 [cited 2023].
     Available from: https://www.collectivefashionjustice.org/under-their-skin

20. Nagesh A. Confessions of a slaughterhouse worker. [Internet]. London: BBC; 2020 [cited 2023].
     Available from: https://www.bbc.com/news/stories-50986683

21. Chavez S. My first job was slitting the throats of chickens at a slaughterhouse. It changed me forever.
     [Internet]. San Francisco: San Francisco Chronicle; 2022 [cited 2023].
     Available from: https://www.sfchronicle.com/opinion/openforum/article/My-first-job-was-slitting-
     the-throats-of-chickens-17017934.php

Animals as nature

1. Holgate B. Microfibre pollution in fashion: are synthetics all to blame?. [Internet].
   Melbourne: Collective Fashion Justice; 2021 [cited 2023].
   Available from: https://www.collectivefashionjustice.org/articles/microfibre-pollution-in-fashion-are-synthetics-all-to-blame

2. Carrington D. Microplastics found in human blood for first time. [Internet].
   London: The Guardian; 2022 [cited 2023]. Available from: https://www.theguardian.com/environment/2022/mar/24/microplastics-found-in-human-blood-for-first-time

3. TEDx Talks. Animals and the climate crisis: a missing perspective I Ryuji Chua I TEDxWarwick.
   2022 [cited 2023]. Available from: https://www.youtube.com/watch?v=xz3jIu6SjXo

4. Legal personhood factsheet. [Internet]. Sydney: Voiceless; c2023 [cited 2023].
   Available from: https://voiceless.org.au/schools/legal-personhood/legal-personhood-factsheet/

5. Conventional cotton. [Internet]. Melbourne: Collective Fashion Justice; 2022 [cited 2023].
   Available from: https://www.collectivefashionjustice.org/conventional-cotton

6. Our story. [Internet]. New York: Nonhuman Rights Project; c2023 [cited 2023].
   Available from: https://www.nonhumanrights.org/our-story/

7. Roy E. New Zealand river granted same legal rights as human being. [Internet].
   London: The Guardian; 2017 [cited 2023]. Available from: https://www.theguardian.com/world/2017/mar/16/new-zealand-river-granted-same-legal-rights-as-human-being

8. Torres-Spelliscy. The history of corporate personhood. [Internet]. New York: Brennan Center for Justice; 2014 [cited 2023]. Available from: https://www.brennancenter.org/our-work/analysis-opinion/history-corporate-personhood

9. Quiggin J. Property rights, corporate personhood and nature. [Internet].
   Turner (AU): Green Agenda; 2019 [cited 2023].
   Available from: https://greenagenda.org.au/2019/04/corporate-personhood/

10. Gratanni M, Sutton S, et al. 'Indigenous environmental values as human values.'
    Cogent Social Sciences. 2016. 2: 1. https://doi.org/10.1080/23311886.2016.1185811

11. Indigenous land rights. [Internet]. Melbourne: Collective Fashion Justice; 2022 [cited 2023].
    Available from: https://www.collectivefashionjustice.org/indigenous-land-rights

12. Wang X, Van der Werff, et al. 'I am vs. we are: how biospheric values and environmental identity
    of individuals and groups can influence pro-environmental behaviour.' *Frontiers in Psychology.* 2021. 12.
    https://doi.org/10.3389/fpsyg.2021.618956

13. Martin C, Czellar S. 'Where do biospheric values come from? A connectedness to nature perspective.'
    Journal of Environmental Psychology. 2017. 52. 56-68. https://doi.org/10.1016/j.jenvp.2017.04.009

14. Bousman T, Steg L, et al. 'Measuring values in environmental research: a test of an environmental
    portrait value questionnaire.' *Frontiers in Psychology.* 2018. 9: 564.
    https://doi.org/10.3389%2Ffpsyg.2018.00564

15. Kingsley J, Townsend M, et al. 'Exploring Aboriginal people's connection to country to strengthen
    human-nature theoretical perspectives.' *Advances in Medical Sociology.* 2013. 15.
    Available from: https://www.emerald.com/insight/content/doi/10.1108/S1057-6290(2013)0000015006/full/html

16. Responsibility. [Internet]. London: Ananas Anam; c2023 [cited 2023].
     Available from: https://www.ananas-anam.com/responsibility/

17. Russel M. Hyosung commercialises first bio-based spandex. [Internet]. Bromsgrove: Just Style;
     2022 [cited 2023]. Available from: https://www.just-style.com/news/company-news/hyosung-
     commercialises-first-bio-based-spandex/

Innovation and just transition

1.   Wood B. Abolishing child labor took the specter of 'white slavery' and the job market's near collapse
     during the Great Depression. [Internet]. Melbourne: The Conversation; 2020 [cited 2023].
     Available from: https://theconversation.com/abolishing-child-labor-took-the-specter-of-white-
     slavery-and-the-job-markets-near-collapse-during-the-great-depression-144454

2.   Walker K. What happened to the world's ozone hole?. [Internet]. London: BBC; 2022 [cited 2023].
     Available from: https://www.bbc.com/future/article/20220321-what-happened-to-the-worlds-ozone-hole

3.   Nenquimo N. This is my message to the western world – your civilisation is killing life on Earth.
     [Internet]. London: The Guardian; 2020 [cited 2023]. Available from: https://www.theguardian.com/
     commentisfree/2020/oct/12/western-worldyour-civilisation-killing-life-on-earth-indigenous-
     amazon-planet

4.   Hakansson E, Carter N, et al. Under their skin: leather's impact on the planet. [Internet].
     Melbourne: Collective Fashion Justice; 2022 [cited 2023].
     Available from: https://www.collectivefashionjustice.org/under-their-skin

5.   Amazkin. [Internet]. Lima: Amazkin; c2023 [cited 2023].
     Available from: https://www.theamazkin.com/#

6.   Hakansson E, Gladman S, et al. Under their skin: a just transition beyond leather. [Internet].
      Melbourne: Collective Fashion Justice; 2023 [cited 2023].
     Available from: https://www.collectivefashionjustice.org/under-their-skin

7.   Nanollose creates sweater made from coconut waste. [Internet]. Nantwich (GB):
     Knitting Industry; 2018 [cited 2023]. Available from: https://www.knittingindustry.com/nanollose-
     creates-sweater-made-from-coconut-waste/

8.   Shear destruction. [Internet]. Melbourne: Collective Fashion Justice; 2021 [cited 2023].
     Available from: https://www.collectivefashionjustice.org/shear-destruction

9.   Catano E. How an ex-coal mining town is turning to ecotourism to rebuild its economy.
     [Internet]. London: The Guardian; 2022 [cited 2023]. Available from: https://www.theguardian.com/
     us-news/2022/apr/05/virginia-coal-ex-mining-town-plans-rebuild-economy

10. Muhlke C. Can fashion be profitable without growth?. [Internet]
     New York: The New York Times; 2022 [cited 2023]. Available from: https://www.nytimes.
     com/2022/12/07/business/dealbook/fashion-profitable-growth.html

11. Unsustainable consumption of fashion. [Internet].
     Melbourne: Collective Fashion Justice; 2022 [cited 2023].
     Available from: https://www.collectivefashionjustice.org/mass-consumerism

12. Vivienne Westwood: "be reasonable, demand the impossible". [Internet]. Lisbon: Impossible.
     labs; 2016 [cited 2023]. Available from: https://medium.com/@impossible/vivienne-westwood-be-
     reasonable-demand-the-impossible-8d9473195b08